GLORIOUS
NEW ZEALAND

Photographs
Previous page: Near Queenstown, Central Otago
Pages 2-3 Eyre Mountains, Southland

Chanel Publishers Ltd
PO Box 403, Whangaparaoa

First published by Chanel Publishers Ltd 2003
© Copyright Chanel Publishers Ltd
Photography: Contributors List Page 200

Publisher: Cliff Josephs
Editor: Linda Cassells
Design: Chanel Publishers Ltd
Production Manager: Barbara Nielsen
Printed by Midas Printing (Asia) Ltd in China

ISBN 0-9582441-0-3

GLORIOUS
NEW ZEALAND

TEXT BY ALISON DENCH

CONTENTS

NORTH

ISLAND

NORTHLAND &
AUCKLAND

Cradle of a Nation

The northern tip of New Zealand offers a study in contrasts – between the flash and dash of Auckland and the quiet isolation of old northern settlements, the eastern coast's peaceful havens and the storm-lashed western shore, the tourist buzz of the Bay of Islands and the relative simplicity of Far North rural life.

Over the centuries the area has drawn more people to it than any other in New Zealand. Maori settlers found its subtropical climate, rich marine life and bird-filled forests irresistible. Early European arrivals were attracted by the sheltered anchorages and fertile soils of the Bay of Islands, and the welcome of local Maori. Even today the city of Auckland, by far the largest in New Zealand, draws migrants from all over the country and the world. The Northland and Auckland regions are home to many of the indigenous people of New Zealand, with nearly one-third of the country's Maori living here. While many dwell in the cities, many others live in the more remote areas of the Far North, including the eerily beautiful Hokianga Harbour on the west coast.

Before settlement of the land began 800 to 900 years ago, Northland and Auckland were covered in a unique combination of kauri and hardwood forest edged by mangrove swamps and dune land. Since then the landscape has changed beyond recognition. Cities and towns have sprung up and spread, forests have been all but destroyed by logging and many of the swamps have been drained – but the sand remains in the never-ending beaches and dunes of the Far North right up to Cape Reinga.

The Bay of Islands, enjoying a prime position on the meandering eastern coastline, is the cradle of New Zealand history. The historic associations are obvious in the spiritually important pa sites of Kororipo and Ruapekapeka, and at Kerikeri in the oldest building in the country, Kemp House.

A little further down the coast the old-world atmosphere of Russell, formerly Kororareka, belies its rougher origins as the notorious 'hellhole of the Pacific'. And across the water from the nation's first capital is the reserve at Waitangi, where the founding treaty between Maori and Pakeha was signed. Long a favourite holiday destination, the Bay of Islands throbs with tourist activity throughout the year. It lures visitors with its historic attractions, its 150 exquisite islands and its opportunities for boating, dolphin swimming, deep-sea fishing and diving.

Further south, among innumerable volcanoes, beaches, bays, headlands and islands, the metropolis of Auckland sits astride the Tamaki Isthmus. Its population is small by world standards, but Auckland's urban sprawl rivals cities like Los Angeles and London. Very much New Zealand's 'big smoke', it has a reputation for fine food, brash residents and high living. It's a city that knows how to relax, with one of the highest rates of boat ownership in the world and dozens of golf courses peppering the city. A wide range of cultural influences – particularly from the Pacific Islands and, more recently, Asia – only adds to the feeling of vibrancy.

Despite their distinctive differences, the Northland and Auckland regions are not always quite as they appear. While Auckland may seem to be a city trapped in gridlock, it's easy enough to escape to the wilderness of the west coast, to the sanctuary of the peaceful islands of the Hauraki Gulf, to the playground of the Mahurangi Peninsula, or deep into the inland forests. And while Northland has been thought of as something of a backwater, today avocado, olive and macadamia orchards as well as vineyards have joined the traditional citrus orchards – and you can find espresso coffee if you look for it.

PREVIOUS PAGES (6–7) Wairarapa farmland; (8–9) The golden sweep of Maitai Bay graces Northland's Karikari Peninsula.
ABOVE According to Maori lore the spirits of the dead depart from Cape Reinga, Northland. RIGHT At Cape Reinga a lighthouse keeps watch over the northern tip of New Zealand, where the Tasman Sea and the Pacific Ocean crash together.

ABOVE Te Paki, Northland. Ninety
Mile Beach is backed by huge sand-dunes
that give the area a distinctly Saharan feel —
and are ideal for tobogganing. Around Te
Paki Stream there are 7 square kilometres
of dune land.

RIGHT The kiwi, New Zealand's
national bird, has been around for about
30 million years. It's a biological oddity,
in many ways more like a mammal than a
bird: it has very poor eyesight but a highly
developed sense of smell, it burrows in the
ground, it has whiskers, its feathers are
more like hair and it can't fly. The
nocturnal bird does, however, lay eggs —
huge ones up to 20 per cent of the weight of
the female.

LEFT *Maitai Bay, Northland.*
The Far North of New Zealand has a halo of sandy beaches that are deserted for most of the year, and the horseshoe-shaped Maitai Bay is one of the most beautiful.

BELOW *Coopers Beach, Northland.*
Doubtless Bay has a number of beach resorts, among them the pohutukawa-fringed Coopers Beach. The spectacular pohutukawa tree is a familiar sight along the coastline of the northern half of the North Island. It is also known as the New Zealand Christmas tree, because stunning spiky red balls of flowers decorate the tree in early summer each year. Doubtless Bay got its name from a note in Captain Cook's logbook: he remarked that it was 'doubtless a bay'.

ABOVE Whale Bay, Bay of Islands.
The crystal waters of remote Whale Bay are
a favourite playground for boaties.

LEFT Kerikeri, Bay of Islands.
Designed and built by missionaries starting
in 1832, the well-proportioned Georgian-
style Stone Store is the oldest building in
New Zealand made of stone. Nearby is the
wooden Kemp House (begun in 1818), the
oldest building in the country. Kerikeri, one
of the first bases for the pioneering Church
Missionary Society, has the longest history
of continuous occupation by Europeans of
any town here.

RIGHT Urupukapuka Island, Bay of
Islands. The sheltered waters of the Bay
of Islands, dotted with 150 islands, lure
visitors from all over the world. Among the
pleasures to be enjoyed are sailing, game
fishing, swimming with dolphins, scuba
diving, snorkelling, sea kayaking, or simply
relaxing on the beach in one of the
hundreds of picturesque, undeveloped coves.

ABOVE Waitangi, Bay of Islands.
It was on the lawn in front of the Treaty House (then the home of British Resident James Busby) that the Treaty of Waitangi, New Zealand's founding document, was signed on 6 February 1840 by Lieutenant-Governor William Hobson and 45 Maori chiefs. The Treaty, under which the chiefs seemed to cede sovereignty to the British Crown, has been the subject of confusion and controversy ever since.

RIGHT Waitangi, Bay of Islands.
Nga Toki Matawhaorua, *one of the largest war canoes in the world, was carved from three massive kauri trees to mark the centenary of the signing of the Treaty of Waitangi. It has its own intricately carved shelter (right) on the Waitangi National Reserve. Every year on Waitangi Day the 35-metre canoe is relaunched – with 80 Maori paddlers on board – to celebrate the anniversary of the signing.*

ABOVE Russell, Bay of Islands.
Originally Kororareka, Russell was the first capital and largest town in New Zealand in the 1830s. Populated largely by whalers, sealers, deserters, recently released convicts and prostitutes, it gained a reputation as a rough neighbourhood. In 1844 and 1845 Maori chief Hone Heke defied the British by four times cutting down the flagpole at Russell before launching a devastating assault on the settlement. The rebuilt town is now a quaintly historic seaside resort and a base for game-fishing boats.

LEFT Russell, Bay of Islands.
When in 1841 Marist missionaries built a structure to house their printing presses they used the rammed-earth construction familiar to them from their home district of Lyon, France. Since 1913 the building has been known as Pompallier House after the bishop who led the mission, although he never lived there. It has recently been restored to its original state.

TOP Piercy Island, Bay of Islands. *The waters of the Bay of Islands are filled with life, including as many as 57 species of fish, as well as dolphins and whales. Fishing from charter vessels tends to be productive, with kingfish, kahawai and snapper quite easily found, and game fish such as marlin (above) and mako sharks providing a bigger challenge.*

ABOVE Mimiwhangata Bay, Northland. *The beach at Mimiwhangata, south of the Whangaruru Harbour, was once one of many substantial Maori settlements along the Northland coast. Today it is part of the Mimiwhangata Coastal Park and a popular spot for forest and farm walks, exploring the cliffs and headlands, and lazing on the beach.*

RIGHT Waipoua Forest, Northland. *The three greatest kauri giants in the country grow in Waipoua Kauri Park. Kauri are among the oldest, largest trees in the world, living for up to 2000 years, growing to 50 metres tall, and developing a girth of as much as 16 metres. About 1.2 million hectares of kauri forest blanketed the northern North Island – until Maori started burning it off for gardens and European settlers took to felling it for its fine, straight timber. Today only a few remnants of untouched forest remain.*

LEFT *Mangawhai Heads, Northland.*
Kilometre upon kilometre of sandy surf beaches attract holidaymakers to Mangawhai Heads, south of Whangarei. Like many New Zealand beaches, Mangawhai's can be dangerous for swimmers and in summer volunteer lifeguards patrol part of the beach. Once a quiet little resort town, in the last few years Mangawhai Heads has boomed and the growing town now has a liberal sprinkling of shops, restaurants and galleries.

ABOVE *Mahurangi, Auckland. Once thought to be too warm and humid for quality winemaking, the districts north of Auckland are now producing premium wines. Boutique wineries, some with their own cafés or restaurants, specialise in red varieties such as Merlot, Cabernet Sauvignon, Syrah, Pinotage, Pinot Noir and Sangiovese, although Chardonnay and Pinot Gris grapes are also grown.*

BELOW *Wenderholm Regional Park, Auckland. Every warm weekend Auckland families flock to the region's beaches and parks for a few hours of rest and relaxation. Just north of the metropolis of Auckland, the beach, the shady picnic areas and the scenic walking tracks of Wenderholm Regional Park offer one such haven from the stresses of city life. The huge plane trees at the entrance of the park mark the original driveway of historic Couldrey House.*

LEFT Waiheke Island, Auckland.
The sheltered waters of the Hauraki Gulf Marine Park, off Auckland, are dotted with 47 islands. At Waiheke Island, one of the biggest and the most developed, it's possible to relax on a picturesque beach, wander around a gallery or two – and stop at one of the island's winery restaurants. Diners at the Mudbrick Restaurant can enjoy a sensational view to the city over grapevines, farmland and the Hauraki Gulf.

BELOW LEFT Rakino Island, Auckland. Aucklanders love to get out on the water whenever they can, and the Hauraki Gulf's islands provide a multitude of anchorages for boats that range from fishing dinghies to multi-million-dollar yachts and launches.

BELOW LEFT Auckland city. The buzzing Viaduct Harbour in downtown Auckland was once the most run-down part of the waterfront. But when New Zealand won in the America's Cup in 1995, all that changed. The old basin was dredged and transformed into a combination of marina for racing yachts and visiting superyachts, and public space for strolling, eating and drinking.

FOLLOWING PAGES Waitemata Harbour, Auckland. Known as New Zealand's 'City of Sails', Auckland is dominated by the salt water that almost entirely surrounds it: the Tasman Sea to the west, the Pacific Ocean to the east, and the two harbours that bite deeply into the narrow peninsula. With a population that is more than New Zealand's other five main centres put together, Auckland is a vibrant and exciting place with a paradoxically laid-back feel. Forty per cent of the city's population was born elsewhere, and Auckland has an intriguing mix of cultural influences – European, Pacific Islands, Maori and Asian. The Auckland Harbour Bridge, opened on 30 May 1959, spans the Waitemata Harbour.

ABOVE Piha, Auckland. The most accessible of Auckland's west coast surf beaches is Piha. The sand here is a startling black, thanks to iron-oxide ash washed up the coast from the Taranaki volcanoes. Less than a century ago the village was a mill town, processing kauri trees from the Waitakere Ranges and sending the timber to a wharf via a 14-kilometre railway that clung tenuously to the coast. Today many surfers flock to the beach, ever watchful of its notorious rips.

RIGHT Muriwai, Auckland. There are few places where it's easy to get close to a gannet colony, and the Takapu Refuge is one of them. From July to October Australasian gannets nest on the island of Oaia, as well as on a rock stack close to shore and the mainland itself. By the end of summer the chicks are ready for an extraordinary first journey – never before having fed themselves or been airborne, they launch themselves on the 2000-kilometre flight to Australia.

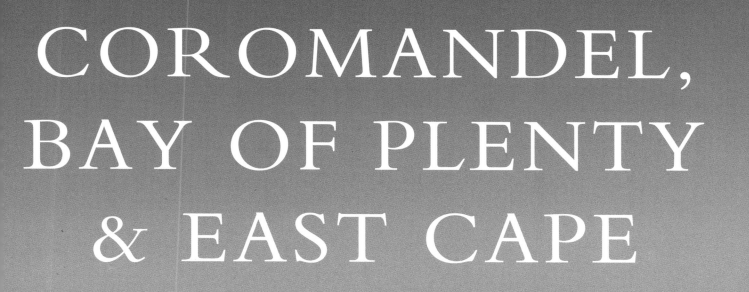

COROMANDEL, BAY OF PLENTY & EAST CAPE

Land of Plenty

Over the peaceful Coromandel, down the sun-soaked Bay of Plenty shore and around the dramatic East Cape, the Pacific Coast Highway affords an unparalleled view of a diverse and intriguing part of the North Island.

After heading south from Auckland, the highway takes the long route up and around the unspoiled Coromandel peninsula. It's well worth the detour — the west coast, facing onto the sheltered Firth of Thames, is shrouded in pohutukawa trees that blossom in a crimson blaze of glory in early summer, while the east coast is a paradise of pristine white-sand beaches. The eastern towns have long been the perfect holiday destination for beach bunnies, swimmers, surf-casters, divers, surfers and boaties.

In the interior the wild forests of the ranges are haunted by the past. From the early 19th century the hills rang with the crashing sound of giant kauri trees being felled for timber. Kauri-gum diggers picked through the remains, then in 1866 the peninsula swarmed with prospectors. But today Coromandel artists and craftspeople exploit only the patterns and colours of nature as inspiration for their work.

From the Coromandel the Pacific Coast Highway curves south-east with the Bay of Plenty. Here beaches and blue sea, rainforest and rolling farmland, warm climate and sunny skies draw visitors and permanent residents alike, and fruit-growing and timber plantations have brought prosperity.

Tourism is another major source of income, especially inland at Rotorua, where naturally heated mineral-rich waters burst to the surface. The government developed Rotorua as a spa town in the 1880s, and more than a century later visitors still flock to this strange-smelling centre. Where else can they explore some of the most easily accessed hot springs, geysers, mud pools and silica terraces in the world, as well as learn about Maori life and culture?

Back on the coast, the highway sweeps on through kiwifruit orchards to thread its way between the East Cape's rough hills and the coves of its shoreline. This is a place apart, where life is lived at a more relaxed pace. Inland from the cape the sacred peak of Hikurangi is each day the first land in the world to be touched by the sun. Nearly half the people in the region are Maori, and Ngati Porou holds such sway that the tribe lent its name to the East Coast's premier rugby team.

The Pacific Coast Highway trundles on through the major city of the East Coast, Gisborne. It was here that in 1769 Captain Cook became the first European to set foot in Aotearoa. Fertile river flats and flourishing vineyards defy the name he gave the district, Poverty Bay. In fact the disenchanted navigator named it so because, he wrote, 'it afforded us no one thing we wanted' — the first encounters with Maori had been bloody and no provisions were secured.

Maori resentment of the intrusion of the Pakeha is a feature of history all around here. For decades almost the only European settlers were missionaries in Tauranga, and many of the East Coast chiefs refused to sign the Treaty of Waitangi. During the New Zealand Wars much of the region was a hotbed of rebellion, and it wasn't until the 1870s that things calmed down enough for the rather Victorian city of Gisborne to be laid out and settled.

Just as well, then, that times have changed and modern visitors are assured of one of the warmest welcomes they are likely to receive in New Zealand.

PREVIOUS PAGES *In the far north of the Coromandel Peninsula, remote Port Jackson overlooks the Hauraki Gulf.*
ABOVE *The Mercury Islands off the Coromandel are a yachting, fishing and diving paradise.* **RIGHT** *The beach at Hahei is acre upon acre of golden sand.*

ABOVE Waiau Falls, Coromandel.
The gold and silver miners tore up the land
and the kauri loggers tore down the forests,
and the Coromandel was left a barren
backwater. Now it has found a new kind
of gold – tourism – and the forests are
regenerating and the streams flow clear again.

RIGHT Cathedral Cove, Coromandel.
At low tide a great arched cavern gives
access to a magical white-sand beach at
Cathedral Cove. The diverse and exciting
sea life in the area is protected by a
marine reserve.

LEFT *Hot Water Beach, Coromandel.*
During the summer holiday season hordes
of holidaymakers descend on the low-rise
beach resorts that dot the eastern coast of
the Coromandel. Hot Water Beach has a
special quirk – thermal water bubbles up
through the sand and holidaymakers can
hire a shovel from the local store to dig
their own low-tide spa pool.

LEFT *Mount Maunganui, Bay of Plenty.*
The lone volcanic cone of Mauao offers a spectacular view of the resort town of Mount Maunganui and the white sandy surf beach and clear blue sea that make it such an appealing holiday destination. Life was not always so peaceful here: it took many years for Europeans to become welcome in the Bay of Plenty. For a long time the only settlers tolerated were the missionaries and traders who set up shop at Tauranga, and during the New Zealand Wars coastal Bay of Plenty was a hotbed of Maori resistance to the British.

BELOW *Tauranga, Bay of Plenty.*
Almost a century ago a Wanganui schoolteacher called Isabel Fraser returned from a trip to China with some small black seeds. These 'Chinese gooseberries' thrived in New Zealand but it wasn't until the 1920s that they were grown commercially, and the 1960s that the vitamin-rich fruits, renamed 'kiwifruit', took off internationally. Today the warm sun and fertile soils of the Bay of Plenty nourish five-sixths of the more than 60 million trays of kiwifruit — both green and gold forms — grown every year in this country.

ABOVE *Rotorua, Bay of Plenty. Now home to the Museum of Art and History, the Tudor-style bath house at Rotorua opened in 1908. The government-owned bath house – the 'Great South Seas Spa' – used mineral waters from thermal springs to treat everything from piles to 'kidney mischief'. Over the years the corrosive water took its toll on the structure of the building and in 1966, with the value of hydrotherapy being questioned, the spa ceased operation. The museum grounds, complete with croquet lawns and wild hot pools, were gifted by local Maori 'for the benefit of the people of the world'.*

MIDDLE RIGHT *Rotorua, Bay of Plenty. Before the Department of Tourist and Health Resorts developed Rotorua as a spa town, the nearby Maori village of Ohinemutu was the base for tours to the world-renowned Pink and White Terraces of Lake Rotomahana. These dramatic silica terraces were destroyed in the 1886 eruption of Mount Tarawera. One of 35 marae in the district, Te Papaiouru at Ohinemutu is the home of the superbly ornamented Tamatekapua meeting house*

FAR RIGHT *Rotorua, Bay of Plenty. Wood carving (whakairo) is an ancient Maori art form. The wooden framework of meeting houses is usually carved with representations of tribal ancestors, and important canoes and household items are also decorated. At the Maori Arts and Crafts Institute in Rotorua visitors can watch carvers at work.*

BOTTOM RIGHT *Rotorua, Bay of Plenty. An integral part of the Rotorua experience is a hangi meal and Maori concert. At a number of hotels, tourist villages and marae, visitors can view the intimidating haka up close (right), as well as enjoy traditional songs and demonstrations of poi twirling.*

LEFT Rotorua, Bay of Plenty. *Rotorua has several volatile geothermal areas, where the weak crust of the earth is so thin that the superheated groundwater breaks through. Among the spectacular features is Waiotapu's colourful Champagne Pool (top left), where boiling alkaline water bubbles to the surface. Walkers must take care where they tread – the very ground below bubbles and boils, slurps and plops, in pools of mud.*

ABOVE Rotorua, Bay of Plenty. *The spectacular Pohutu Geyser at Whakarewarewa sends a jet of steam and boiling water up to 30 metres into the air. Sometimes it plays only intermittently, at other times it throws up its scalding stream continuously for months or even years at a time. Either way, it's one of the most famous geysers in the world, entrancing tourists for a century. The Maori name Pohutu means 'splashing'.*

BELOW White Island, Bay of Plenty. A little over 50 kilometres off the coast from Whakatane lies White Island. Whakaari, to use its Maori name, is New Zealand's most consistently active volcano. It's actually three separate volcanic cones arranged around a large crater that belches dense clouds of steam. The smouldering, roaring island also oozes sulphuric acid and exhales toxic gases from fumaroles, and the scientists who come from all over the world to study the volcano must take care to protect themselves.

RIGHT Mata River valley, East Cape. High above the crumpled hills and winding valleys of the Raukumara Range, the sacred peak of Hikurangi is the first place each day on the mainland to be touched by the sun. While farmland has extended from the coast into the foothills, much of the range is covered by dense bush and the only people who penetrate its darkest recesses are hikers, hunters, fishers and whitewater paddlers. According to Maori tradition, Hikurangi is the resting place of Nukutaimemeha, the waka (canoe) from which ancestral hero Maui fished the North Island out of the sea.

ABOVE *Tokomaru Bay, East Cape.*
The coast road around East Cape is
punctuated by a number of small,
predominantly Maori settlements where the
horse is part of everyday life, a hangover
from a time when the only way to travel
around the cape was by sea or on horseback.

RIGHT *Anaura Bay, East Cape. In*
1769 Captain James Cook and the crew of
the Endeavour *rediscovered New Zealand*
after Abel Tasman's first sighting more than
125 years earlier in 1642. They came first
to the east coast of the North Island, and
one of their early landfalls was in beautiful
Anaura Bay. At that time heavy bush
covered the area, with some land cleared by
Maori for large gardens on the flat lands
close to the sea, but today farmland and a
reserve flank the tiny settlement.

ABOVE *Tolaga Bay, East Cape. The longest wharf in New Zealand, and possibly the Southern Hemisphere, stretches 660 metres into Tolaga Bay. Its beginnings were inauspicious: miscalculations and heavy seas hampered construction and the wharf took four years to complete. When it was at last officially opened in 1929, the event was marred when four women dangling their legs from a rail wagon had them crushed. Despite problems with maintenance the wharf served the coastal shipping trade for nearly 40 years. The pier was a lifeline to farmers at a time when it was impractical to transport local meat and wool by roads that were unsealed. Ships no longer berth here, but the restored wharf is still used by recreational boats, walkers and fishers.*

RIGHT *Young Nicks Head, Poverty Bay. On his 1769 voyage on the* Endeavour, *Captain James Cook offered a gallon of rum and naming rights to the first crew member to sight New Zealand.*

The prize went to the 12-year-old surgeon's boy, Nicholas Young, whose fresh eyes were able to make out the white bluffs that Captain Cook then named Young Nicks Head.

FAR RIGHT *Gisborne, Poverty Bay. The first Europeans in Aotearoa (the Maori name for New Zealand) made landfall at Turanganui-a-Kiwa, modern Poverty Bay, in 1769. Sadly the first encounter between Maori and Pakeha was fraught and quickly turned violent. On Kaiti Hill a statue of the expedition leader, Captain James Cook, commemorates the event. Cook, who made three trips to New Zealand, discovered more of the earth's surface than any other person.*

LEFT AND ABOVE *Te Urewera National Park. The largest tract of untouched forest wilderness in the North Island can be found in Te Urewera National Park. The ancient podocarp and beech forest (left) and the mist-veiled mountains are the spiritual home of the Tuhoe tribe, 'The Children of the Mist', the offspring of Hine-puhoku-rangi. Much of the park is not easily accessible – during the New Zealand Wars many Maori rebels found refuge in its remoter tracts – but the mysterious and moody Lake Waikaremoana (above) and the lush bush that surrounds it can be explored on a popular track. The 46-kilometre Lake Waikaremoana Track is one of the 'Great Walks', nine routes maintained by the Department of Conservation to a particularly high standard.*

WAIKATO, CENTRAL PLATEAU & TARANAKI

Heart of the Island

From the plains of the Waikato, through the tortured hills of the King Country, to the mountains of Taranaki and Tongariro National Park, great rivers and mighty volcanoes determine the nature of the central western region of the North Island.

First among the rivers is the Waikato. The longest river in New Zealand roars out of Lake Taupo, over the Huka Falls and through nine hydro-electricity stations. Further down its course the Waikato meanders gently through silt plains and marshland – and the region's major city, Hamilton – to the Tasman Sea, feeding and watering one of the world's most prosperous dairying, agriculture and thoroughbred areas as it goes.

The second great river is the Whanganui, which rises on the western flanks of Tongariro and carves a winding path to the sea at Wanganui. The Whanganui was for centuries the best way to Taupo and the central volcanoes, and until road and rail links opened up the region in the first part of the 20th century, steamer trips into the the wild heart of the North Island were a major tourist attraction. Today the river through Whanganui National Park has been left to recreational canoeists, kayakers and jet-boaters.

The Whanganui was also once the only route through the dense forests and broken hills of the King Country. The area got its name after members of the Maori King Movement took refuge in its dark corners after being driven out of the Waikato by the land-hungry British in the 1860s. At Waitomo visitors today take advantage of the somewhat easier access allowed by state highways to take in the breathtaking wonders of the limestone caves – many of them still uncharted – and their shimmering glow-worms.

The cluster of mountains that commands the centre of the North Island is a World Heritage Area. Tongariro National Park was gifted to the nation by Ngati Tuwharetoa chief Te Heuheu and in 1894 became only the second national park in the world. The most impressive of the park's volcanoes are Ngauruhoe, Tongariro and Ruapehu – the last of which is thronged with skiers, snow-boarders and climbers in winter, despite the fact it could erupt at any time.

The park marks the western end of the Taupo Volcanic Zone, where the Pacific tectonic plate slips beneath the Indo-Australian plate. Lake Taupo, New Zealand's largest lake, fills the caldera formed by successive eruptions, including one in AD230, the most violent eruption on earth in the last 5000 years. Today the place is more tranquil, offering world-class trout fishing on the lake and the cool, clear streams that empty into it – although hot springs and bubbling mud pools are present reminders of past violence.

Separated from its fellow volcanoes in the central North Island by 150 kilometres, Mount Taranaki utterly dominates the province it gave its name. It is a spiritual icon for both Maori and Pakeha New Zealanders. Its near-perfect cone, often surrounded by a halo of cloud, forms the backdrop to every local vista, be it of subtropical forests, rich pastures or wild surf beaches.

The Taranaki region was once described as 'The Garden of New Zealand', and with its regular rainfall and soil fertilised by volcanic ash early European settlers found it ideal for dairy farming – at the expense of vast tracts of native forests as well as the local Maori people, who were forced out. More recently Taranaki has gained a new nickname, 'The Energy Province', since natural gas was discovered at Kapuni in 1962, and later offshore, and oil was struck east of the mountain in the 1980s. Like much of the area covered in this chapter it has recently emerged from a dark period of decline to bask in the warmth of an economic boom.

PREVIOUS PAGES Mount Ruapehu presides over the Central Plateau. *ABOVE* Mount Taranaki, also called Mount Egmont, gave its name to both a Maori tribe and a province. *RIGHT* The Waikato River runs through the green heart of a prosperous farming region.

ABOVE   Hamilton, Waikato. Until 1879 the only link between the rival settlements of Hamilton East and Hamilton West was the unreliable punt service across the Waikato River. Now a number of bridges span the river, including since 1937 Fairfield Bridge.

ABOVE   Hamilton, Waikato. The largest inland city in the country, Hamilton was named after Captain John Hamilton RN, a British war hero who was killed at the battle of Gate Pa in 1864. A defensive military settlement was built on the site of the village of Kirikiriroa after British troops had driven Maori out of the area during the Waikato War, and soldiers were paid with blocks of farmland confiscated from Maori as 'punishment' for resisting British rule. Once simply a provincial farming service town, Hamilton has seen spectacular recent growth and is becoming more cosmopolitan by the minute. The city hosts a number of festivals and national events, including Balloons over Waikato in which hot-air balloons from all over the world float away in a stunning spectacle.

RIGHT   Matamata, Waikato. Some of the finest thoroughbred racehorses to come out of New Zealand have been bred and trained in the Waikato. One of the secrets of their success is the easy availability of lush, green, year-round pasture on gently rolling hills.

ABOVE Waikato. Every last scrap of usable land in the Waikato, be it scrub, swamp or forest, has been converted to farmland, and much is dedicated to feeding dairy cows. Since the end of the 19th century, when the dairy industry became mechanised and farmers banded together into co-operatives, the Waikato has been the 'dairy bowl' of New Zealand — and the world. New Zealand first exported dairy products in 1846 — a shipload of cheese to Australia — with the first refrigerated export coming in 1882. In the 2000/01 season the dairy industry processed more than 12.3 billion litres of milk from 3,485,883 cows in 13,982 herds, more than one-third of them in the Waikato.

ABOVE AND LEFT Raglan, Waikato. The beaches at Raglan, on the west coast of the Waikato, are a drawcard for the world's discerning surfers. Manu Bay (above), often called 'The Point', is reputed to have the longest left-hand break in the world, and regularly produces exceptional waves. Surfing first took off in New Zealand in 1958, after two visiting US lifeguards rode their boards at Piha, near Auckland, and it's still all the rage up and down the country. Raglan town — surfers call it 'Rag Town' — is a small, relaxed seaside resort, with craft shops, cafés and a sheltered harbour perfect for kayaking, windsurfing and swimming.

FOLLOWING PAGES Waitomo, King Country. The name says it all. Scattered around the Waitomo area are dozens of vertical shafts (tomo) that descend into deep, dark, dank cave systems with underground streams (wai) running through them. These awe-inspiring caves are created by a formula of subtraction and addition: acid rainwater dissolves the limestone, scouring out the tomo and caves, then deposits the limestone again as it drips from stalactites to stalagmites, on helictites and flowstones. The result is an other-worldly place where weird natural sculptures abound and where night and day collide, with the only light supplied by constellations of luminous glow-worms. The three show caves of Waitomo, Ruakuri and Aranui are open to the public and can be explored on foot, by boat — or bobbing around in a truck tyre inner-tube.

ABOVE *Taupo, Central Plateau.*
Above Huka Falls the mighty Waikato
River, the outlet of Lake Taupo, suddenly
narrows through a cleft in the rock before
dropping 11 metres in a rush of churning,
foaming blue water. It's a clear
demonstration of the raw power that drives
nine hydro-electricity stations further
downstream.

RIGHT *Turangi, Central Plateau. The*
Tongariro River, which flows into Lake
Taupo at its southern end, is famous among
the world's fly fishers for its fat, vigorous
trout, particularly the winter spawning runs
of rainbow trout. The fish were introduced
at the end of the 19th century, and the
Tongariro is now so productive that anglers
have to queue to cast a fly.

ABOVE ***Taupo, Central Plateau.*** *Lake Taupo and the streams that feed it are stocked with trout both through natural means and by a carefully managed hatchery. Anglers rate the Waitahanui River, which rises in the hills east of the lake and runs through the settlement of Waitahanui, as one of the best streams in the area.*

LEFT Taupo, Central Plateau. In a restrained mood on a still autumn day Lake Taupo is tranquil, but it is fickle — when a stiff wind blows the ripples become white-caps and the lake can become almost menacing. At 616 square kilometres, the largest body of water in New Zealand seems big enough to be called an inland sea.

BELOW Taupo, Central Plateau. Above a serene Lake Taupo the volcanic cones of Mounts Ruapehu and Ngauruhoe are a reminder of a more violent past. Lake Taupo, now popular for the laid-back pursuits of boating and fishing, lies in a depression left about 1800 years ago by one of the most destructive series of volcanic eruptions in recorded history. An earlier eruption, 26,500 years ago, was one of the largest ever to occur on earth.

ABOVE Tongariro National Park, Central Plateau. *The name Tongariro originally encompassed all three of the majestic volcanoes that rise suddenly into the clear air above the central North Island. It refers to the prayer of Maori explorer Ngotoro-i-rangi who, caught out at the top of the mountain, called on the fire gods to send him warmth: 'Ka riro au i te tonga! ('I am carried away by the bitter south wind!'). The gods sent underground fire that burst through at*

Whakaari (White Island), Rotorua, Tarawera, Paeroa, Orakei Korako, Taupo and, at last, from the mountains around Ngotoro-i-rangi. The 2797-metre Mount Ruapehu, the perfectly conical Ngauruhoe and the smaller peak of Tongariro beyond are all considered active. The crater lake of Ruapehu is an indicator of brewing volcanic activity, and when the acid water changes colour or starts steaming it is sending us a warning signal.

LEFT Tongariro National Park, Central Plateau. Thousands of years ago Mount Ruapehu, the highest mountain in the North Island, stood dramatically higher than it does today but huge avalanches have truncated its cone. This unstable giant last lived up to its name ('exploding crater') in 1995, when in a terrifying display of the earth's power the crater erupted, sending ash, water and huge boulders into the sky and muddy lahars down the river valleys.

ABOVE Tongariro National Park, Central Plateau. The establishment of New Zealand's first national park around the three great mountains of Tongariro was made possible by a gift of the land from the Tuwharetoa people in 1887. At the foot of Ruapehu, in the heart of the starkly beautiful park, is the Grand Chateau. This neo-Georgian hotel opened in 1929 to accommodate tourists during the early days of skiing at Whakapapa and today it offers a taste of old-style hospitality to snow lovers, hikers and sightseers.

LEFT Tongaporutu, Taranaki. For kilometre upon kilometre south of the hamlet of Tongaporutu, the white cliffs of Parininihi form a bastion against the surging Tasman Sea. A walking track through the Whitecliffs Conservation Area affords some remarkable views.

BELOW New Plymouth, Taranaki. The city of New Plymouth, the main centre of Taranaki, provides easy access to the many natural attractions of the province: surfing at one of the numerous local beaches, walking in the dense forests of Egmont National Park, climbing to the icy 2518-metre peak of Mount Taranaki, and skiing on its lower slopes.

LEFT *Whanganui National Park, Wanganui. The Whanganui River, which winds from Mount Tongariro through the King Country and Wanganui, has a remarkable place in New Zealand history. According to legend the course of the river was gouged by Taranaki as he fled Tongariro after a feud, and early Maori used it as canoe route to Taumarunui. After European settlement steam-powered riverboats plied its scenic canyons. Land around the river was allocated to servicemen returning from World War I, but much of the rough, hilly country proved unsuitable for agriculture. By the 1930s most of the farmland upriver had been abandoned, the steamers had stopped running, and the Whanganui returned to its natural state of peace. Now that a national park has been formed around the river, and a paddling trip down its rapid-peppered waters declared one of New Zealand's 'Great Walks', it bustles with human life again.*

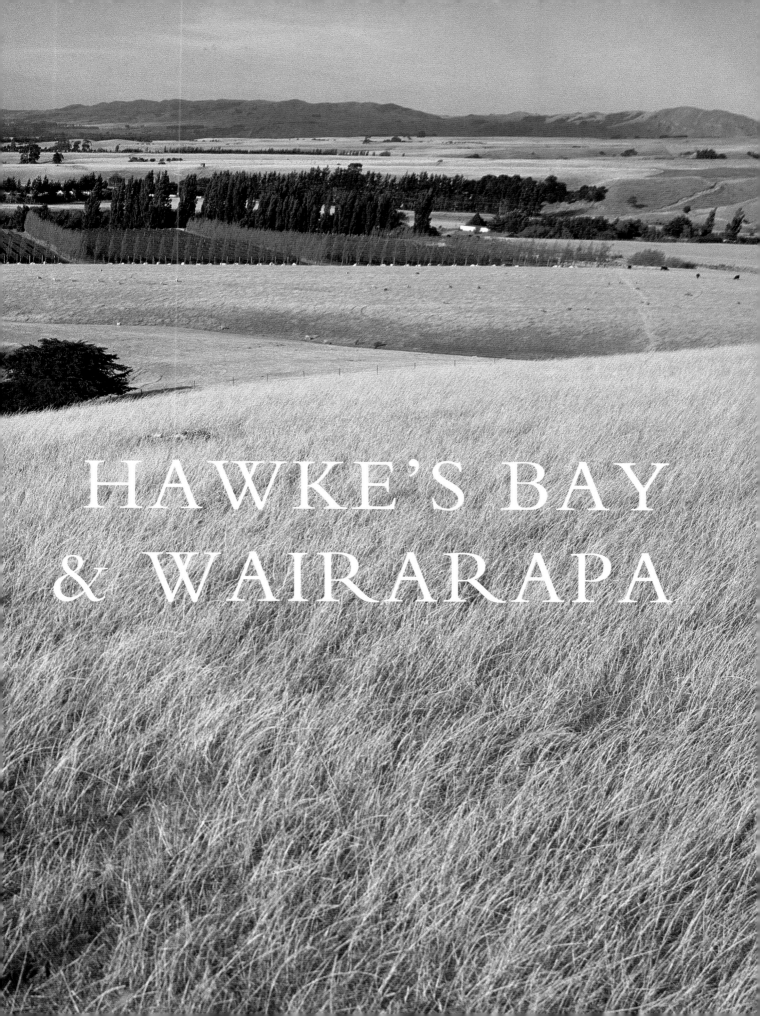

HAWKE'S BAY & WAIRARAPA

Slice of Life

Sandwiched between the mountainous spine of the North Island and the relentless Pacific Ocean, a green sliver of farmland, much of it pasture, runs from Hawke's Bay right through to Cook Strait. But each part of the sliver has its own unique character.

In the north, Hawke's Bay has a distinctly Mediterranean feel. It's in the weather — mild winters and hot, dry summers — and in the Spanish Mission architecture and the hillsides of olive groves. And it's in the acres of vineyards. If there's one thing that gives the region an allure that's desperately hard to resist, it's the award-winning wines produced there.

At the heart of this wine-lover's paradise are Napier and Hastings, where city and country converge. As the twin towns have grown and touched tentacles, they have not merged identities. Napier, the original provincial capital, is the business centre with a busy port, while Hastings is the hub of the prosperous rural sector and home to vast food-processing factories handling the fine produce of the orchards and market gardens of the fertile Heretaunga Plain.

Both cities have a uniformity in their architecture, a result of carefully planned rebuilding after an earthquake in 1931 devastated the region and left hundreds dead. With so many new buildings being constructed in the style that was all the rage at the time, Napier has become the art deco capital of the world, and today's shoppers and sightseers find themselves surrounded by streamlined buildings decorated with chevrons, sun bursts and ziggurats. Hastings and Havelock North went their own way, tending more to the Spanish Mission style.

Wheeling and diving at the southern tip of the bay, beyond endless kilometres of wild beaches, over the summer months the gannets of Cape Kidnappers give a dramatic display of precision hunting. To the west the darkly forested bulk of the Ruahine Range looms as an ever-present backdrop to the less intimidating meadows of sheep and dairy farms.

Further south, the Wairarapa seems to be one vast model New Zealand farm — clean air, lush green fields and millions of sheep. For many years after European settlement began the difficulty reaching the region from Wellington through the Rimutaka Range meant development was slow. That all changed in 1855 when a massive earthquake raised land from the sea bed and made it much easier to travel along the shoreline. By the 1860s the new settlers had established large sheep stations in the style of those in Australia. Although sheep farming was the main economic provider for a century and a half, today many of the stations have been subdivided and the land is also used for deer farming, horticulture and forestry.

When road and rail links forced their way through the Rimutaka Range in the 1870s a string of towns sprang up along them. Once considered a little sleepy for city tastes, some of them have become 'lifestyle' towns where jaded Wellingtonians go for a weekend retreat or even to retire. Prime among these is Martinborough, right in the heart of Pinot Noir country, where visitors can explore the many vineyards by bicycle. Greytown, with its historic buildings and excellent cafés and restaurants, has its own unique appeal.

Remote from the main highway, Wairarapa's dramatic coastline stretches bleakly between two capes named by Captain Cook — Turnagain and Palliser. Along the southern coastline the tiny fishing villages that dot the edge of Palliser Bay experience the worst the Cook Strait gales have to offer, and many lives have been lost in shipwrecks. The coast of southern Wairarapa, only a couple of hundred kilometres away in distance, is a million kilometres away in spirit from the orchards and vineyards of balmy Hawke's Bay.

PREVIOUS PAGES The quiet hills ripple into the distance in rural Wairarapa. *ABOVE* Te Mata Estate in Hawke's Bay makes some of the most admired wines in New Zealand. *RIGHT* A sculpture celebrating the 'Spirit of Napier' graces the waterfront.

ABOVE AND RIGHT   Napier, Hawke's Bay. In 1931 a massive earthquake all but razed the colonial seaside town of Napier, and killed 256 people throughout the region. When it came to the rebuilding, young architects looked for inspiration to the slick, stripped-back art deco style, shunning the dangerous masonry cornices and parapets that had struck so many in the quake. The people of Napier have proudly preserved their unique architectural heritage and today their city has the most complete collection of art deco buildings in the world. Among the signature buildings are Hotel Central (above), designed by E. A. Williams, and J. A. Louis Hay's Ellison & Duncan building (right).

ABOVE Hawke's Bay. *In spring the Heretaunga Plain lights up with the blossom of fruit trees. Hawke's Bay is known as the 'Fruit Bowl of New Zealand', producing about half of New Zealand's apple crop and up to 70 per cent of the peaches, nectarines, plums and apricots. Pears, kiwifruit and grapes are also grown.*

LEFT Ngatarawa, Hawke's Bay. *Winemaking has been a feature of Hawke's Bay life since 1851, when the first vines were planted by Marist missionaries at Pakowhai. The climate is ideal for grape-growing – cool enough that the grapes ripen slowly, retaining their subtle flavours, but warm and dry enough to suit late-maturing red varieties such as Cabernet Sauvignon. The vineyards of Ngatarawa Wines (left) produce a range of both red and white wines under the watchful eyes of fourth-generation New Zealand winemakers, the Corbans.*

ABOVE   Hastings, Hawke's Bay. In the middle of a fertile plain, Napier's twin town of Hastings services a thriving horticultural sector. The prosperity that has come from the orchards and market gardens helped fund the extensive Windsor Park, with its water park, children's playgrounds, tennis courts, sports fields and duck-friendly lake, all shaded by stately English trees.

RIGHT   Havelock North, Hawke's Bay. The Tukituki River rises high in the Ruahine Range and flows east through the dry hills and green river flats of the back country into Hawke Bay.

BELOW   Raukawa, Hawke's Bay. Sheep are a very important part of the economy of both Hawke's Bay and New Zealand as a whole, and the national flock contains about 40 million sheep — about 10 for every human being. Sheep farming began with some of the earliest European settlers, but did not really take off until refrigerated shipping services began in 1882 and frozen New Zealand lamb could be exported to the world.

LEFT AND BELOW
Cape Kidnappers, Hawke's Bay. *At the southern end of Hawke Bay, Cape Kidnappers was named by Captain Cook after local Maori tried to kidnap a Tahitian crew member from the* Endeavour. *To Maori the cape is Te Matau-a-Maui ('the fish-hook of Maui'), after the hook with which Maui, the ancestral hero, fished up the North Island from the sea. Over spring and summer thousands of Australasian gannets rear their chicks on the bare sandstone outcrops of the promontory. In March the chicks fly off to the east coast of Australia where they remain until they become adults, and at three to six years old they return to New Zealand waters for good. Many do not survive the perils of the journey – less than one-third of these fascinating seabirds make it home again.*

ABOVE Waipawa, Hawke's Bay. The forbidding Ruahine Range, a constant presence in Hawke's Bay, is part of the spine of the lower North Island. The steep, rugged terrain offers some of the best, most challenging hiking in the North Island. The range is in Ruahine Conservation Park, part of the more than 5 million hectares – over one-third of the nation's total land area – administered as parks by the Department of Conservation.

LEFT Kairakau Beach, Hawke's Bay. Remote Kairakau Beach is one of a small number of settlements far from the main road on the coast south of Cape Kidnappers. Permanent residents, holiday-makers and bach-dwellers share the open beach and take advantage of the good surf-cast fishing. A bach (referring to bachelors) is a weekend house or cottage, traditionally small and basic with outdoor facilities but these days increasingly likely to be large and architect-designed with all mod cons.

*RIGHT Wairarapa. Though some of
the stockyards may be tumbledown, the
southern Wairarapa is still very much sheep
country. It's been that way since 1844,
when Charles Bidwill brought the first flock
around the coast from Wellington,
piggybacking them one by one through the
surf at Mukamuka rocks.*

LEFT   Castlepoint, Wairarapa. Breaking the monotony of the windswept Wairarapa coastline is Castlepoint, a popular seaside resort where a jagged rocky reef protects a sandy lagoon and the swimming is safe and the surf-casting productive. The Castle Point lighthouse, built in 1913, casts its warning light 50 kilometres out over the Pacific Ocean, greeting ships making the long voyage to Wellington from the United States and Panama. Like all New Zealand lighthouses it is no longer manned – instead it is controlled by 'mouse power' from a computer in Wellington.

FAR LEFT   Martinborough, Wairarapa. Once notable as the site of the first sheep station in New Zealand, Martinborough is now better known for its Pinot Noir grapes and gourmet foods. Palliser Estate is among more than 20 boutique vineyards making the most of the sun-baked, free-draining loamy soil to produce award-winning wines.

BELOW LEFT   Martinborough, Wairarapa. Martinborough Wine Village, as the marketers like to call it, is a favourite weekend destination for Wellingtonians looking for a relaxed country retreat. The recently restored Martinborough Hotel, lucky to have escaped the fires that destroyed so many early wooden buildings around the country, has hosted visitors in varying degrees of colonial elegance since 1882.

FOLLOWING PAGES   Cape Palliser, Wairarapa. The lighthouse at Cape Palliser stands on the south-eastern tip of the North Island high above a rocky and gale-torn coastline that saw many lives lost in early shipwrecks. The stormy shore does offer excellent fishing, however – something not lost on the residents of the nearby seal colony, the largest in the North Island.

MANAWATU & WELLINGTON

Rural Retreat and Cultural Capital

The country's busiest road, State Highway 1, may run right through the middle of the Manawatu on its way to Wellington, but this region feels like it's off the beaten track. On one level, the region offers the clichéd vision of New Zealand – fertile fields sprinkled with woolly sheep and plump dairy cattle. On another level, it is still undiscovered country.

The rural idyll was not easily won. When the first would-be squires arrived from Europe, they found forests, swamps, scrub and dune land – and local Maori wisely not straying far from the river banks. Over the next 60 years thousands of settlers hacked, burned and drained the landscape into the pleasant and unthreatening pastures of today. But there is much more to Manawatu than farming. During lean times many farmers diversified into tourism, offering everything from visits to historic homesteads and gardens to adventure tourism.

In the inland hills, the Rangitikei is an untamed river of exceptional beauty, running clear and fresh under imposing white siltstone cliffs. Over on the coast, you can get lost in New Zealand's largest dune field, and at Foxton one of the country's most important estuarine ecosystems, with 2000 birds of 58 species, awaits exploration. Now just a small township, Foxton was once a busy port and the centre of a thriving flax industry. But the main trunk line of the railway bypassed the town and the tidy and perhaps a little conservative university city of Palmerston North ('Palmie' to its friends) has become by far the biggest in the region.

If the Manawatu is known for its 'old money', Wellington is more about 'new money'. The capital city has a relatively young and transient population, and it is here that some of the best educated and highest paid people in New Zealand get together

to run the country – at Parliament and in the fine buildings of the finance district.

Wellington is the city that never should have been. When the New Zealand Company, the agency that was the organising force behind European settlement, selected the site, it noted only the excellent deep-water harbour and turned a blind eye to the contours of the land. The result is a city hemmed in by hills, crammed precariously on ridges and in gullies, with steep, winding roads. The developers also glossed over the fact that it's right on top of a fault line and subject to frequent earthquakes.

Proud Wellington was known at first as the 'Empire City'. It seems to attract nicknames – it is also referred to as the 'Windy City' for the gales that regularly howl through Cook Strait. To be fair, though, between days of driving rain Wellington has its share of beautiful, calm, clear days, and since Peter Jackson made the *Lord of the Rings* films here, some prefer to call it 'Wellywood'.

In recent years this city of bureaucrats has reinvented itself as a tourist destination. Wellington has a vibrant arts scene, and the International Festival of the Arts is a biennial bonanza for culture vultures. The remarkable national museum called Te Papa Tongarewa is a drawcard for New Zealanders and overseas visitors alike. And food lovers are sure to find something to please the palate in the cafés and restaurants of Courtenay Place.

As the city has grown it has sprawled beyond the hills. Despite hard times for farmers, the Kapiti Coast – opposite the Kapiti Island bird sanctuary – is thriving as it has become a popular sunny retirement spot and, even as far as Waikanae, a commuter zone for the capital. It looks like an age-old trend is reversing, and the city is moving back to the country.

PREVIOUS PAGES Matiu or Somes Island, in Wellington Harbour, was once a quarantine station – and a camp for enemy aliens during World War II. ABOVE Wellington's distinctive 'Beehive' houses the executive offices of parliament. RIGHT Poplar shelterbelts protect the pastures of Awahou North, Manawatu.

LEFT Palmerston North, Manawatu.
*The gardens, lawns and fountains of the
Square mark the centre of Palmerston
North. The provincial city was not always
the major centre for the region – it was only
when the railway bypassed the port town of
Foxton, heading inland instead to
Palmerston North, that 'Palmie' came into
its own. In a reflection of its site in the
middle of very productive farmland, the city
is home to Massey University, which since
1927 has been central to the study of
agricultural science in New Zealand.*

LEFT Pohangina River valley,
Manawatu. The river flats around the
Pohangina are among the most intensively
farmed land in New Zealand, and since the
1870s, when hard-working pioneer farmers
felled and burned the dense virgin bush,
sheep have proved a very valuable asset.

BELOW Horowhenua coast,
Manawatu. New Zealand's largest dune
field stretches almost unbroken for 200
kilometres from Paekakariki all the way north
to Patea. The flat, sandy beaches of the west
coast provided an important route for Maori
and early European settlers, part of a pre-
railway 'main trunk line' that continued up
the Whanganui River to Taumarunui and
the Central Plateau. North of Foxton Beach
the dune field reaches several kilometres
inland, before the Tararua Range rises
abruptly from the plain.

LEFT, ABOVE AND BELOW   Kapiti Island, Wellington. Brooding Kapiti Island is a sanctuary for native birds where all introduced animals, from possums to goats, have been eradicated. The island, 6 kilometres off the coast north of Wellington, was a defensive stronghold of Maori military leader Te Rauparaha – the man whose haka has been adopted by New Zealand sports teams – in the 1820s. It was a base for whalers and then a farm, but since 1897 its wind-blasted western hillsides and sheltered eastern rainforests have been set aside as a nature reserve. Kapiti Island has been replanted in native vegetation and is now a haven for a colourful parrot, the kaka (below), as well as many bird species that are rare or even extinct on the mainland, including the little spotted kiwi, takahe, kakariki, robin, bellbird, stichbird and saddleback. To prevent the return of predatory pests to the island, while the sanctuary is open to the public, access to Kapiti Island Nature Reserve is by permit only and numbers of vistors are limited.

RIGHT   Paekakariki, Wellington.
The beach settlements of the Kapiti Coast,
once holiday areas and retirement homes,
have become commuter suburbs of
Wellington. Residents of Paekakariki enjoy
a milder climate than Wellington's, as well
as surfing, swimming and fishing from the
sandy beaches, paragliding and hang-gliding
from the hills that rise to the east, and
walking or riding in the dunes and coastal
forest of Queen Elizabeth Park to the north.

ABOVE Brooklyn, Wellington. *High above the centre of the capital city, in the teeth of the gales that regularly blast through, a turbine at an experimental wind farm converts Wellington's most common element into electricity. The 'Harbour City' is a centre for the arts, and home to the country's parliament, the national museum and library, and the national headquarters of many organisations.*

LEFT Island Bay, Wellington. *South of the city Island Bay, once an outlying settlement, is now a suburb. The island, Taputeranga ('sacred island'), was a refuge for Maori, but in the late 19th century Island Bay became a seaside resort for Wellingtonians. In the early 20th century a number of Italian and Shetland Islands fishermen settled here, and the Italians in particular have retained a distinct cultural identity.*

FAR LEFT *Oriental Bay, Wellington.*
A house with sea views isn't that unusual in Wellington, where even the steepest hills have been built upon, but Oriental Bay, with its beach and boat harbour, is a sought-after suburb. Some homes have private cable cars to hoist people, as well as the weekly shopping, up from the road.

ABOVE *Lambton Harbour, Wellington.*
The nation's treasures are held in the modern Museum of New Zealand, Te Papa Tongarewa. The museum prides itself on its high-tech interactive exhibits as well as more traditional galleries. The building has state-of-the-art shock absorbers that protect it from the earthquakes that occasionally strike the city.

LEFT *Lambton Harbour, Wellington.*
The capital city has very little naturally flat land, and much of the downtown area has been built on land reclaimed from the harbour. It is an area for walkers, who find the government precinct, the business centre, restaurants, theatres and the waterfront all within strolling distance.

RIGHT Cook Strait. The Interislander ferry service links the North and South Islands – although it actually travels north from Wellington to reach Picton. The ferries must negotiate Cook Strait, one of the wildest and most unpredictable stretches of water in the world. In 1968 freak winds blew the Wahine *ferry off course and it was wrecked at the entrance to Wellington Harbour with the loss of 51 lives. Modern ferries are specially designed for the crossing and can sail in all but the worst conditions.*

SOUTH

ISLAND

NELSON & MARLBOROUGH

Graced by the Sun

The most northerly regions of the South Island are blessed with snow-capped mountains, sunny beaches, turquoise waters and emerald forests. With three national parks and any number of smaller parks and conservation areas, Nelson and Marlborough are a kind of paradise for anyone who wants to get away from it all right in the heart of New Zealand.

The early Maori settlers, attracted by the mild climate, sheltered harbours and rich sea life, may not always have felt so blessed. When Abel Tasman arrived at Golden Bay in 1642 bringing first contact with Europe, local Maori were suspicious and attacked the strange visitors, killing four of the crew of the *Zeehaen*. Over the centuries that followed there were successive waves of invaders from the North Island, each tribe wiping out the traditions and history of the last.

By the time the colonisers of the New Zealand Company, planning a new large city, finally selected the site – even as the first settlers were en route from England in 1841, Nelson's future location was still uncertain – few Maori lived in the northern part of the South Island.

European settlement had a very shaky start. The new arrivals didn't have the skills or the money to make a go of it, and soon found themselves enduring a famine. Then in 1843 came the deaths of 22 of Nelson's finest citizens in a confrontation with a Maori war party that became known as the 'Wairau Affray' and soured race relations for decades.

Part of the region's salvation came with the arrival of two ship-loads of hard-working German immigrants who brought with them grapevines and hops. Their influence is still felt today. Nelson and Marlborough have gained a reputation as wine and beer producers and Blenheim's Sauvignon Blancs are renowned.

The two major towns of Nelson and Marlborough have their own distinctive flavours. The biggest and oldest, Nelson is an exciting small city with a sense of history. It's the home of a lively and progressive community of artists, and a perfect reflection of Nelson's love of the arts and the off-beat is the annual Wearable Art Awards, in which everything from food to copper wire is used to make art that can be worn.

Blenheim, half the size of Nelson and in the middle of the Wairau Plain, gets its sense of identity more from farming and the marvellous wines produced nearby. The annual highlight is creative in its own way: at the Marlborough Food and Wine Festival dozens of winemakers and gourmet food producers take the chance to show off their fare.

This is very much a region for foodies. The fruit trees of Nelson blaze with blossom in spring, growers sell local olive oil, cheese and honey at their gates, and Marlborough aquaculture – Greenshell mussels, oysters, salmon, paua (abalone) and freshwater crayfish – keeps the economy thriving. But the greatest resource of Nelson and Marlborough is quite natural and untouched. It's the water, the wilderness and the weather.

For centuries the inlets of the Marlborough Sounds have offered shelter to travellers, and today the maze of waterways and slivers of land between them are a haven for sailors, kayakers, walkers, fishers and bikers. Golden granite-sand beaches and beech forests make Abel Tasman National Park a magnet for hikers and paddlers. The lakes and mountains of Nelson Lakes National Park are a hiker's and skier's dream. The conservation area of Farewell Spit is a treat for bird lovers. And all of this can be enjoyed in a climate of long summers, mild winters and sunshine so plentiful it rates as New Zealand's sunniest region.

Nelson and Marlborough – and the visitors who are lucky enough to travel there – are indeed blessed.

PREVIOUS PAGES (100–101) *Mount Cook, overlooking Lake Pukaki;* **(102–103)** *The sun rises on another glorious day in Pelorus Sound, one of the many fiord-like valleys of the Marlborough Sounds.* **ABOVE** *The sea at Totaranui, Abel Tasman National Park, is an invitingly clear blue-green.* **RIGHT** *The nature reserve of Farewell Spit curves away from the north-western tip of the South Island.*

LEFT *Abel Tasman National Park, Nelson. Anchorage Bay is a stopping-off point for both yachts and walkers on the Abel Tasman Coast Track, one of New Zealand's most popular multi-day walks. The track meanders around the coast between Marahau and Wainui Bay, along pristine golden-sand beaches, past seal colonies, and up and over headlands covered in beech forest.*

ABOVE *Wainui, Nelson. Deep in the beech forest of Abel Tasman National Park, the Wainui River rises on the slopes of Mount Evans, then makes its way north to Wainui Inlet. Along the way it carves through broken gorges and thunders over the atmospheric Wainui Falls.*

*RIGHT   Abel Tasman National Park,
Nelson.* Miles down a dusty, winding
road, remote Totaranui and its busy
campground are best reached on foot via the
Abel Tasman Coast Track or the water
taxis that service the bays and beaches of
New Zealand's smallest national park.
Whatever the arching sweep of the beach at
Totaranui might suggest, the district of
Golden Bay got its name not from the
picture-perfect beaches but from a gold strike
in the Aorere River in 1857. Before that,
Europeans had known the bay itself as
Murderers Bay, after Dutch explorer Abel
Tasman and four of his crewmen were killed
by surprised and alarmed Maori in 1642.

RIGHT *Kaiteriteri, Nelson. More accessible than the secluded beaches of Abel Tasman National Park, Kaiteriteri is a well-loved family beach resort, one of the most popular in the South Island. In 1841 Captain Arthur Wakefield, agent for his brother Edward's New Zealand Company, considered Kaiteriteri for the site of the Nelson township but he eventually settled on a site across Tasman Bay.*

BELOW *Abel Tasman National Park, Nelson. Birds throng the forests and shores of Abel Tasman National Park. The woodlands are home to bellbirds, fantails, kereru (New Zealand pigeons) and tui, sandy estuaries like that at Awaroa provide the ever-changing habitat ideal for wading birds, gannets, shags and terns, and blue penguins have burrows on the offshore islands.*

*ABOVE Mapua, Nelson. With its
waterside cafés and galleries, the small port
of Mapua, at the entrance to the Waimea
River estuary and once primarily a farming
and industrial settlement, has created a new
niche for itself.*

*RIGHT Tahunanui, Nelson. The beach
at the Nelson suburb of Tahunanui – locals
call it simply 'Tahuna' – is a hive of
activity in the summer months. Holidaymakers can swim in the safe waters of the
bay, play beach volleyball, try kitesurfing,
rent a bumpa boat, take up windsurfing, fly
a kite or hurtle down a hydroslide.*

*BELOW Port Nelson. Well known for
its exciting arts and crafts, including the
Wearable Art Awards, the city of Nelson is
the hub of a fruit-growing and winemaking
district. North of the city centre, Port
Nelson is being developed to take full
advantage of its prime location and
panoramic views over Tasman Bay.
Restaurants have opened, the pub has been
upgraded and apartments have been built,
making it a destination in its own right.*

ABOVE AND LEFT Nelson Lakes National Park, Nelson. Lake Rotoroa (above) and Lake Rotoiti (left), which fill depressions gouged by ancient glaciers, are both accessible by road and thus popular for fishing, yachting and swimming. The mountains and valleys around them are well-tracked hiking country. The luxuriant beech forest hums with bird life, including the country's smallest bird, the rifleman, while at higher altitudes snow tussock and alpine herbs fight for survival among the craggy rock and loose scree. The fenced Rotoiti Nature Recovery Project aims to create a predator- and pest-free refuge for native wildlife. While a number of New Zealand's offshore islands have had similar schemes for years, this is one of the first 'mainland islands' for species recovery.

ABOVE Kenepuru Sound, Marlborough Sounds. In the Marlborough Sounds densely forested ridges extend like fingers into flooded river valleys, creating a maze of coves and inlets, peninsulas and islands. It is a yachting and kayaking paradise, though paddlers must be wary of treacherous currents and punishing winds. Roads have not reached much of the coastline, so many homes and farms rely on boats for transport.

RIGHT Queen Charlotte Sound, Marlborough Sounds. Queen Charlotte Drive, a scenic route that snakes along the southern shore of Grove Arm and past Governors Bay (right), has delightful views of the sandy coves and dramatic headlands of the Sounds. Sheltered Queen Charlotte Sound was an old Maori trade route, and gold and antimony miners, whalers, fishermen, farmers, foresters and now tourists have all found something of value to them in the area. The Queen Charlotte who lent her name to the sound, the road and, across the other side of the water from Governors Bay, the walking track was the consort of George III, the king of England at the time Captain Cook visited the Sounds and gave this one its name.*

LEFT Queen Charlotte Sound, Marlborough Sounds. The 71-kilometre Queen Charlotte Track offers walkers and mountainbikers a multi-day adventure through undisturbed native forests and along skyline ridges with breathtaking vistas of complex waterways all around, including the Bay of Many Coves (left). Early European explorer Captain Cook made Ship Cove, at the northern end of the track, his base in New Zealand.

BELOW **Picton, Marlborough.** *Picton Harbour, an arm on the south side of Queen Charlotte Sound, is the terminal for the ferries that cross to and from Wellington many times a day. Once a gold-rush boom town but now a peaceful service town for tourism, farming, fishing and shipping, Picton came close to replacing Auckland as the country's capital during the 1860s but narrowly lost out to Wellington.*

RIGHT *The unique tuatara has been around for 220 million years, since the time of the dinosaurs. Half of New Zealand's tuatara ('spiny back') live on Stephens Island in the northern Marlborough Sounds. The lizard-like reptiles do everything slowly: they take up to 35 years to reach their full size of about 50 centimetres, and their eggs take nine months to form and 11 to 16 months to hatch.*

ABOVE Blenheim, Marlborough. One of New Zealand's most successful wine regions, Marlborough is world famous for its crisp Sauvignon Blancs, sophisticated Rieslings and delicate sparkling wines. Montana Wines (above) was the first to see the potential of this, the driest and sunniest of the winemaking regions, and planted the first vines in 1973. Other large wine companies followed, but it was the boutique wineries like Hunter's and Te Whare Ra that first captured the world's attention. Today Marlborough is the biggest wine region in New Zealand, with more than 50 wineries and over 5000 hectares of bearing vines. Grape growing is concentrated on the Wairau Plain around Blenheim, but it has spread south to the Awatere valley too. Delegat's is one of a number of wine companies regularly winning awards around the world for Marlborough wines, some made from grapes grown in the Oyster Bay vineyard (right). Marlborough Sauvignon Blanc is so highly regarded that it has become the benchmark for the style, the standard by which winemakers all over the world measure their success.

KAIKOURA &
CANTERBURY

Landscape of Contrasts

On a good day the Canterbury province can provide everything you might hope for in a New Zealand picture postcard: snow-dusted mountains, a glacier or two, rivers braiding through fertile plains, mobs of sheep artfully clustered on the rolling foothills, a genteel colonial city and even dolphins frolicking off the coast.

The single biggest region in the country does seem to have it all. In the north, on the boundary with Marlborough, the tiny fishing port of Kaikoura has seen settlement as long as humans have been in Aotearoa. Today it is renowned as one of the best places in the world to watch — and even swim with — those most admired of marine mammals, whales and dolphins.

South of Kaikoura State Highway 1 takes a tortuous route over the parched hill country of North Canterbury before being released into the vast expanse of the Canterbury Plains. Here the great rivers that descend from the Southern Alps have left behind the silt and gravel they have ground away from the mountains to create one of the biggest shingle fans in the world.

The plains, an obvious choice for European settlement, were at first ignored in favour of hilly Banks Peninsula. A ship-load of French emigrants set out for Akaroa in 1840 and it looked for a moment as if the South Island might become a French colony — but by the time they arrived the Treaty of Waitangi had given Queen Victoria sovereignty over the whole country.

When the English landed ten years later to make Christchurch their home they found it easier than many other settlers. They had geography going for them — flat land is an excellent start — and disputes with Maori were minimal because Ngai Tahu, the main tribe of the South Island, had been almost completely destroyed first by internal battles and then the raids of North Island tribes.

The Church of England settlers built an English Gothic town before spreading out with their sheep runs into the plains, the foothills of the Alps and eventually the high country. Within 11 years there were 877,000 sheep in Canterbury and today sheep farming is still an essential part of the region's history and economy.

The development of pasture meant clearing the forests of the Canterbury foothills, forests where the extraordinary moa once ranged. The only birds in the world to have no wings, these ostrich-like creatures were as much as 2 metres tall at the shoulder. Moa provided an excellent food source for the earliest of Maori settlers between 800 and 1000 years ago — but were hunted to extinction within a few hundred years.

From Christchurch an old Maori route reaches through the Alps via the dramatic mountain scenery of Arthur's Pass. Now a masterpiece of modern engineering with its tunnels and viaducts, the original road was hacked out with picks and shovels in the 1860s. Further south the Burkes Pass route passes through the Mackenzie Country with its snow-fed rivers, dry and treeless hills, sparkling lakes and iconic views of Mount Cook. Both rate among the country's most enjoyable drives.

History is all around in Canterbury, yet at the same time it's a modern kind of place. Despite its reputation as sleepy and conservative, Christchurch boasts more cafés, restaurants and bars per capita than anywhere in New Zealand, and local produce includes the famous lamb, world-class wines, and a range of gourmet foods.

For many the greatest appeal of Christchurch is its location near the playgrounds of the Southern Alps. It is the easiest thing in the world to fill weekends with energetic outdoor activities like hiking, skiing, climbing and surfing — or, failing that, idly wandering the markets or sitting in the sun at a beachfront café.

PREVIOUS PAGES *The tiny Church of the Good Shepherd overlooks Lake Tekapo, in Canterbury's Mackenzie Country.*
ABOVE *A sperm whale dives near Kaikoura, North Canterbury.* **RIGHT** *The fishing port of Kaikoura, once a whaling and sealing settlement, now reaps the benefits of the abundant marine life through eco-tourism.*

ABOVE **Kaikoura, North Canterbury.**
Kaikoura is a fishing port so seafood is
always on the menu – and the ubiquitous
local speciality is crayfish. It's sold at the
wharf, in restaurants and fish shops and
from roadside caravans. In fact crayfish is so
much a feature of local life it gave Kaikoura
its name, which means 'meal of crayfish'.

LEFT **Kaikoura, North Canterbury.**
The Kaikoura Peninsula, which lies only
20 kilometres from snow-capped mountains
of the Seaward Kaikoura Range, could not
have a more dramatic setting. A colony of
seals has made its home on the rocks at the
seaward end of the peninsula, while paua
(a local version of abalone) can be gathered
from the bays.

ABOVE AND RIGHT *Kaikoura,*
North Canterbury. *The very deep but
sheltered waters off the coast of Kaikoura
teem with nutrients, making it a rich feeding
ground for everything from the crayfish
harvested for centuries by Maori to the
marine mammals and birds that draw
nature-lovers today. Here it is possible to
swim with huge pods of high-spirited dusky
dolphins (above), the acrobats of the dolphin
world, or to view majestic sperm whales
(right) at close quarters. Humpback whales,
orca and the tiny Hector's dolphin (found
only in New Zealand waters), New
Zealand fur seals and magnificent royal
albatrosses are also regular visitors to the
Kaikoura coast.*

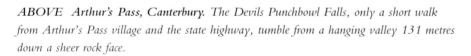

ABOVE Arthur's Pass, Canterbury. The Devils Punchbowl Falls, only a short walk from Arthur's Pass village and the state highway, tumble from a hanging valley 131 metres down a sheer rock face.

RIGHT Arthur's Pass, Canterbury. The alpine village of Arthur's Pass is nestled in the Bealey River valley beneath the towering peaks of the Southern Alps. The national park the settlement serves, straddling the Main Divide of the Alps, is a park of contrasts. On the western side the mountains fall steeply away into the lush, damp bush and roaring rivers of Westland, while the drier eastern side has open beech forests and rivers gently meandering through wide glacial valleys. In summer visitors exploring the ridges and valleys enjoy some of the most spectacular hiking to be found in New Zealand, and winter snow and ice tempt skiers and mountaineers to head for the hills.

FOLLOWING PAGES Canterbury Plains. In the rain shadow to the east of the Southern Alps lies the largest expanse of flat land in New Zealand. Once dry tussock lands buffered the mountains from the ocean, but now for nearly 200 kilometres an orderly grid of farmland stretches north and south as far as the eye can see. In the most modified ecosystem in the country, wheat fields and pastures have been laid neatly over the merged river deltas of the Canterbury Plains. Their margins are defined by dead-straight roads, and shelterbelts that shield them from high winds coming down the foothills.

LEFT *Christchurch, Canterbury.*
Capital of a province once described by Mark Twain as 'Junior England', Christchurch is most English of all. When the first English settlers, who arrived in 1850, dug their new home out of the swamp they set out to recreate the home they had left behind. At the heart of the prim market town they built Christchurch Cathedral, the proud focus of a precinct of historic buildings. Work on the Gothic stone church began in 1864, but funds ran short and it was another 40 years before it was completed. Outside it stands a fine stone-and-bronze memorial, a poignant reminder of the sacrifices made in World War I.

LEFT   Christchurch, Canterbury. *Queen Victoria still reigns happy and glorious over a small corner of Empire in Victoria Square. The tourist tram is a reminder of the time nearly a century ago when Christchurch was criss-crossed by 85 kilometres of tram tracks.*

BELOW LEFT AND RIGHT Christchurch, Canterbury. *The many parks and reserves of the 'Garden City' offer easy respite from the urban bustle. The Avon River (left), lined with exotic trees and shrubs, winds peacefully through the centre of town. In spring, when daffodils bloom among the flowering cherry trees, the Botanic Gardens (right) put on a display to warm the heart after the chilly Canterbury winter.*

PREVIOUS PAGES *Lyttelton Harbour, Canterbury. Christchurch is unusual in having its sea port, Lyttelton, located some distance away from the city over a range of hills. It was in Lyttelton Harbour that the 'pilgrims' of the First Four Ships, the founding settlers of Christchurch, cast anchor – only to be faced with a daunting climb over the Port Hills to reach their destination. The harbour, photographed here at the seaside resort of Governors Bay, is now connected to Christchurch by a 2.4-kilometre rail tunnel completed in 1867 as well as a much more recent road tunnel.*

ABOVE AND RIGHT *Akaroa, Canterbury. The first permanent European settlers in Canterbury were not the English who came to dominate the region, but the French. In 1840 French colonists established a settlement at Akaroa, well out on Banks Peninsula. They arrived a little too late, however, to press a claim for the South Island – just before they got there British sovereignty had been declared. Today the picturesque resort town of Akaroa has a peculiarly Gallic charm, with the locals proud to maintain the French connection. The township sits on the shore of Akaroa Harbour, which, like Lyttelton Harbour on the other side of the folded hills of the peninsula, is a flooded volcanic crater.*

LEFT *Lake Tekapo, Canterbury. First stop for many on a tour of the Southern Alps, the Mackenzie Country's Lake Tekapo gives visitors a first taste of the grandeur of the mountains. In spring and early summer lupins bloom in pinks and mauves on the lakeshore. Pretty though they are, the lupins are not welcomed by all and their days may be numbered – they are exotic invaders that overwhelm native plants and so threaten bird life.*

BELOW *Fairlie, South Canterbury. When by 1855 all the flat land of the Canterbury Plains had been taken up, European settlers moved inland to the rolling, tussock-covered downs. One of the most famous pioneers was James McKenzie, but the 1000 sheep he arrived with turned out to be stolen. He spent nine months in prison (escaping twice) before he was pardoned. His stature, his athleticism, his droving ability and the remarkable talents of his trusty sheepdog Friday have entered New Zealand folklore, and a district, a basin, a pass and a river have all been named after him, albeit with the altered spelling of Mackenzie.*

FOLLOWING PAGES *Lake Ruataniwha, South Canterbury. The mirror-like Lake Ruataniwha, from whose shores rise the lonely hills of the Ben Ohau Range, is a world-class rowing venue and a popular fishing spot. It is part of an extensive chain of lakes, canals and power stations that supply hydro-electric power to both the North and South Islands – and bodies of fresh water perfect for angling for trout and salmon.*

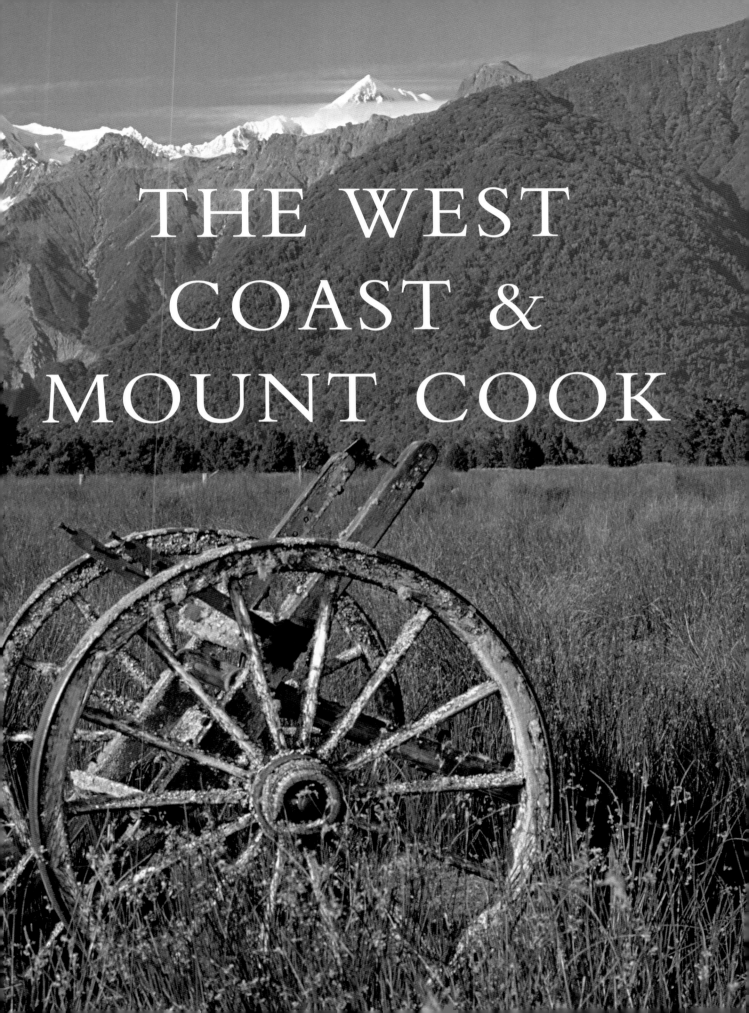

THE WEST
COAST &
MOUNT COOK

Back to Nature

The starkly beautiful West Coast is a place for explorers more than colonists, for sojourners more than settlers. The land Captain Cook described as 'wild, craggy and desolate' has never been exactly welcoming to visitors and, bearing the brunt of the westerly weather systems that storm in from the Tasman Sea, probably never will be.

The swampy estuaries, fast-flowing rivers, dense forests, immense glaciers and celebrated peaks that fascinate visitors today held little appeal for Maori, who used to make the trip across the Alps to collect the treasured pounamu (greenstone). The stone, especially the nephrite jade found in the Arahura River, was hard and gorgeously coloured and much sought after by tribes for making tools and weapons. It gave its name to the South Island, Te Wai Pounamu ('greenstone waters').

Early European settlers, too, found little to interest them – even exploring the extreme terrain seemed impossible – until gold was found near the Taramakau River in 1864. The gold rush that followed brought tens of thousands of hardy hopefuls to the West Coast and kept them there for three years, until the easily available gold had been panned, sluiced or dredged out of the rivers. Not quite all of it was taken, though, and even today there is gold to found in the tailings left behind by the miners.

When the gold ran out the people that remained turned their attention to coal mining and timber, but now that the coal reserves are almost gone and logging of the magnificent indigenous forests has been banned, tourism is the main earner for the ever-adaptable people of the West Coast.

For a landscape so heavily exploited, the West Coast's seems wild and untouched, and with five national parks – or parts of them – within its bounds it is likely to stay that way. From the raw power of the rivers that crash down from the mountains to the sea to the mysterious ambience of the forests, it is nature that enthralls visitors.

At Punakaiki the Pancake Rocks show off the sea's ability as a sculptor, while the smoothed limestone canyons of the interior demonstrate the rivers' talents. Further south at Fox and Franz Josef a short stroll will take you to two of the steepest and most impressive glaciers in the world, while a helicopter ride will give a bird's eye view of these merciless rivers of ice.

The source of the glaciers, the Southern Alps, looms high above the boggy plains and fractured foothills. Above all the rest the summits of Mount Cook and Mount Tasman are a dream destination achievable by accomplished mountaineers only, but the vast snow fields just below are merely a light plane ride away.

In the temperate rainforests native birds flit from branch to mossy branch and sing their entrancing songs. On the bleak and wind-swept coast breathtaking expanses of sandy beach are littered with driftwood and the unrelenting surf pounds the rocky headlands. And in the lagoons and estuaries behind the shoreline unique, undamaged ecosystems await exploration by launch or kayak.

The West Coast is a place of endless change. The rivers scour the mountains away, heavy rain regularly floods the plains, and the glaciers annihilate everything in their path when they advance. The warm, wet climate means that quick-growing scrub and forest have in many places healed over the scars left by mining or logging, but land cleared for farming or gardening can just as easily be reclaimed by nature. The mountain weather is fickle and storms can blow in from the ocean in an instant.

This is not a landscape to be taken lightly, and few Coasters do. It is a dynamic place to embrace nature in one of its wilder forms and to treat it with the respect it deserves.

PREVIOUS PAGES *The highest peaks of the Southern Alps tower over the Fox valley.* **ABOVE** *The tiny Church of St John the Baptist in Westport is part of the Anglican Church, the largest religious sect in New Zealand.* **RIGHT** *The Tasman Sea thrashes the West Coast at Meybille Bay, Buller. The bay is named after a French gold prospector of the 1860s.*

ABOVE Paparoa National Park, Buller. *The soft limestone that underlies most of Paparoa National Park is responsible for its weird and wonderful sculptured landforms – caves, ridges and cliffs, and scoured river canyons like those of the Fox River (above). Lush lowland rainforest covers the inland ranges: northern rata, rimu and miro above a tangle of broadleaf trees, nikau palms, tree ferns and vines. Tui, bellbirds and kereru (New Zealand pigeon) flap from tree to tree, and the great spotted kiwi may be heard but not seen – this shy nocturnal bird makes a snuffling sound or a harsh whistling cry. Within the park there is also a colony of Westland black petrels, the only one in the world.*

ABOVE LEFT Punakaiki, Buller. *The start of the whitebaiting season on the West Coast's rivers is a sign that spring can't be far away. Whitebait are the translucent, wriggly immature stage of various species of Galaxias, and the most common is called inanga. In late winter, having hatched from eggs laid in the lower rivers and spent around 20 weeks at sea, the young fish return to the rivers, looking for bush-covered streams and swamps to settle in – and the whitebaiters are waiting for them with set nets and huge, round scoop nets. Something of a national delicacy, whitebait are traditionally served in whitebait fritters.*

LEFT Punakaiki, Buller. *It's thought the mysterious Pancake Rocks at Punakaiki were formed millions of years ago when alternating layers of mud and lime-rich silt were laid down on the seabed. After earth movements raised the stratified rock, the sea eroded the mud layers more than the limestone, leaving the distinctive stacks of 'pancakes'. At high tide sea water surges around the rocks and through tunnels to explode out of a number of blowholes with a booming sound that echoes around the caverns. The walk to Pancake Rocks must be one of the most popular short walks in the country, attracting upwards of 400,000 people every year.*

LEFT AND ABOVE *Greymouth, Westland. The largest town on the West Coast, Greymouth has a long mining history. Maori treasured the pounamu (greenstone or jade) to be found a little further south in the Arahura River and called the site of the future town Mawhera ('wide-spread river mouth'), but Europeans didn't make an impact until West Coast gold was struck in 1864. The rush was over within three years, but before long more miners moved in to remove the valuable bituminous coal, which was shipped from the Greymouth wharf. Then the emphasis moved on to mining the forests, felling native timber for construction and furniture making. Now that most of the gold has gone, coal production has declined, and logging has been banned, Greymouth is looking to new ventures to sustain it.*

BELOW *Hokitika, Westland. The country town of Hokitika, with its Empire-celebrating clock tower, was established in the mid-1860s with the discovery of gold. In no time at all it had a population of 6000, a number it has never achieved again. 'Hoki', as it's often known, is the country's main centre for working greenstone. For centuries Maori have cut and polished greenstone found on the West Coast to make precious jewellery and weapons, and today artisans all over town use the stone, beautifully coloured yet very hard, to make traditional pendants as well as modern souvenirs.*

LEFT AND ABOVE *Westland/Tai Poutini National Park, Westland.* Fed by smaller glaciers high in the snow fields of the Alps, Franz Josef Glacier (left) and Fox Glacier (above) flow steeply down into rainforest less than 20 kilometres from the sea. These remnants of larger Ice Age glaciers stretch, tumble and groan, and break up into awe-inspiring icefalls of crevasses and pinnacles. They travel up to ten times faster than other valley glaciers, partly because of the angle of the descent, and partly because the Southern Alps catch the prevailing westerly weather and up to 30 metres of snow falls on the névés every year. The great weight of the snow turns it into ice crystals and it flows, under its own irresistible momentum, in a great river of ice. Nowhere else in the world are glaciers so close to the sea at this temperate latitude, nor so easily accessible. Franz Josef and Fox are the most famous of the more than 60 glaciers in Westland/Tai Poutini National Park.

PREVIOUS PAGES Aoraki/Mount Cook National Park. Mount Cook reigns supreme over the Southern Alps. Its Maori name Aoraki is usually translated as 'cloud piercer', giving a clue to the 3754-metre mountain's status as New Zealand's highest. From the shoulder of Mount Cook a string of lesser peaks stretches to the north: first Mount Tasman, then Lendenfeld Peak and, closest to the camera, the rocky Mount Haast. The 3000-metre peaks of the Southern Alps have long been the proving ground for New Zealand's great mountaineers, including Sir Edmund Hillary, the first man to set foot on the summit of Mount Everest.

RIGHT Westland/Tai Poutini National Park, Westland. On still days Lake Matheson is a perfect reflecting pool for the rimu, kahikatea and koromiko forest that fringes it, as well as the mightiest peaks of the Southern Alps, Mount Tasman and Mount Cook. The 'kettle' lake fills a depression left behind thousands of years ago by the retreating Fox Glacier, which once extended all the way to the sea. The neighbouring Westland/Tai Poutini and Aoraki/Mount Cook National Parks are the jewel of Te Wahipounamu World Heritage Area, which protects the fiords, rocky coasts, towering mountains, peaceful waterways and ancient forests of the south-west of the South Island. The kea, the only alpine parrot in the world, lives in the park, as does the endangered takahe, a large flightless bird.

LEFT   Westland/Tai Poutini National Park, Westland. The lush lowland rainforests of Westland thrive in the mild temperatures and heavy rainfall. Tangled tree limbs are clothed in vines, mosses and epiphytes, and ferns make the forest floor almost impenetrable.

ABOVE   South Westland. Some magnificent stands of beech trees grow in Westland, but only where the Ice Age glaciers have not destroyed them. Elsewhere podocarps dominate the forests, with kahikatea (white pine) gracing the wetlands and lake edges and rimu (red pine) making its home on the glacial moraines and old river flats. Southern rata, with its showy red flowers, and kamahi trees grow in the valleys and on the lower slopes of the mountains.

BELOW   Bruce Bay, Westland. North of the tiny settlement of Bruce Bay rimu trees crowd the high tide mark, standing tall against a barrage of salt spray and wild weather. Beachcombers on the wild and exposed shoreline of the West Coast look out for quartz, schist and greenstone along with driftwood battered and scoured into intriguing shapes.

ABOVE *Jackson Bay, Westland. The wharf at Jackson Bay, one of the few natural harbours on the West Coast, serves a commercial fleet that fishes the untamed waters between Greymouth and Bluff. Jackson Bay, with its magnificent views of the Southern Alps, is an end-of-the-road town in more ways than one. At the southern extremity of the West Coast highway, the tiny hamlet is a shadow of its former self, having once been one of the most prosperous Maori villages on the coast and then, for a brief, sodden, scandal-marked time in the 1870s, a pioneer settlement.*

LEFT *Arawata River, Westland. Overlooked by the Haast Range, the Arawata River is one of hundreds of fast-flowing rivers that tumble west from the Southern Alps into the Tasman Sea. This river lent its name to 'Arawata Bill', a prospector and adventurer who died in 1947, only to be immortalised in a sequence of poems by one of New Zealand's finest poets, Denis Glover.*

CENTRAL
OTAGO
& FIORDLAND

New Zealand's Scenic Wonderland

Central Otago and Fiordland are known throughout the world as a holiday resort. It's not surprising – they offer such a range of mesmerising landscapes and rewarding experiences within a relatively small distance. There's enough in just these two regions in the south-west of the South Island to keep the most jaded of travellers happy for weeks.

The deep, dark lakes, imposing mountains and arid tussock uplands of Central Otago, with their freezing winters, scorching summers and difficult access, were inhospitable to Maori, who mostly only stopped off there on the way west in search of greenstone. And it took Nathaniel Chalmers's amazing 1853 journey of exploration, on foot and by a raft made of rushes, to discover its potential and entice Europeans to graze their sheep there.

It was the discovery of gold in the Arrow River in 1862 that lured settlers to Central Otago in their thousands and transformed Queenstown from an isolated farm into a bustling town. Today the remnants of prospecting dreams, scattered around the landscape in ghost towns and abandoned diggings, in the blazing autumn leaves of exotic willow and poplar trees, are poignant reminders of a time when so many were full of hope, and so many disappointed.

When the rush was over most of the miners moved on to the next gold field, but not all the settlements became ghost towns. The southern lakes district, from Hawea in the north to Manapouri in the south, became a favourite summer holiday spot for citizens of Dunedin and Invercargill who, like the visitors of today, soaked up the hot, dry weather and revelled in the opportunities for walking in the sunburnt hills and boating on the tranquil lakes. The rustic lakeside 'cribs' (holiday homes) were soon joined by hotels and motels and, more recently, upmarket bed-and-breakfast accommodation and lodges.

In 1960 Queenstown began to secure its place as a tourist town with the completion of the Coronet Peak ski field in the rugged country north-east of the town. In time it would be joined by others in The Remarkables and, over the Crown Range near Wanaka, Cardrona and Treble Cone. Queenstown became a year-round resort, offering skiing, boating, and walking on the Routeburn and Greenstone Tracks. But it didn't really come into its own until a decade or so later when commercial jet-boats and whitewater rafts started taking adventurers down the Shotover River and, a few years on, A. J. Hackett began his world-first bungy jumping operation. Today Queenstown is a lively and cosmopolitan resort where you can sample award-winning local wines, try your luck in a casino – and take part in any number of extreme sports.

Queenstown is also a jumping-off point for trips to Te Anau, base for a number of dramatic and sometimes demanding walking tracks, and the glories of Milford Sound. Fiordland National Park, which occupies a huge chunk of land on the south-western coast and is part of the Te Wahipounamu World Heritage Area, protects some of the wildest country in New Zealand. In its untouched acres waterfalls tumble from hanging valleys into virgin forests and lakes glitter among the granite peaks.

On the coast, at the end of one of the world's most spectacular drives, lies the gasp-inducing scenery of Milford Sound. This moody and mysterious fiord, with the distinctive Mitre Peak as its mountain sentinel, would have to be New Zealand's most photographed place. Further south the primeval rainforest, cascading waterfalls and unique wildlife of Doubtful Sound are just as impressive as Milford but with a greater sense of solitude and peace, showing that even in New Zealand's busiest tourist region it is possible to get away from it all.

PREVIOUS PAGES *Lonely Macetown in Central Otago is a ghost town dating to the Arrow River gold rush of the 1860s.*
ABOVE *Grapes grown in Central Otago are made into a range of fine wines.* **RIGHT** *Central Otago's Lake Wanaka, hemmed in by mountains, is a year-round holiday destination.*

ABOVE *Lake Hawea, Central Otago.* *The serene lakes of Central Otago, jewels set off by the grandeur of the Southern Alps, are a magnet for vacationers with an outdoors urge. Lake Hawea has an abundance of salmon and brown trout to entice fishers, as well as opportunities for hunting, hiking and skiing in the mountains nearby.*

BELOW *Mount Burke Station, Central Otago.* *On the narrow isthmus between Lake Wanaka and Lake Hawea, Mount Burke Station is one of hundreds of high-country sheep stations in the South Island. In 1853 Nathaniel Chalmers, a young sheep drover, was the first European to see the lakes of Central Otago, and thanks to his*

excited reports of a vast kingdom of grass all the land between Hawea and Manapouri to the south was occupied by sheep runs by 1861.

RIGHT *Macetown, Central Otago.* *In autumn the exotic trees of Central Otago put on a colourful display that takes the breath away. The trees in Macetown were planted by settlers who first came here in the late 1860s in search of gold. The population quickly reached 3000 but within 50 years the gold had run out and the remote town was deserted. All that remains today are a few tumbledown stone cottages and lone chimneys – and the trees and flowers planted by hopeful gold miners.*

ABOVE *Queenstown, Central Otago.*
The vineyards of Central Otago, among
them Chard Farm, are New Zealand's
highest-altitude vineyards and the world's
most southerly. Pinot Noir is the stand-
out style.

LEFT AND RIGHT *Queenstown,*
Central Otago. Once a gold rush town,
Queenstown today offers a rush of a
different kind – adventure tourism. Since
the 1970s Shotover Jet has offered high-
speed thrills in the locally invented jet-boat
(right), and in the 1980s bungy jumping
from the Kawarau Bridge (left) started a
craze that spread all over the world. Among
the dozens of outdoor adventure activities
available are everything from the sublime
(hot-air ballooning) all the way to the
ridiculous (river sledging).

LEFT *Queenstown, Central Otago.*
Below the gondola station on Bobs Peak,
Queenstown sprawls over its site beside
Lake Wakatipu and in the shadow of the
Remarkables range. The town is barely
recognisable from its beginnings as a service
town for gold miners and sheep farmers,
although a few historic buildings have been
preserved and runholders from the valleys do
still mingle with the tourists.

BELOW *Queenstown, Central Otago.*
The self-styled 'adventure tourism capital
of the world' does have a more sedate side.
Since 1912 the historic steamship TSS
Earnslaw *has cruised Lake Wakatipu*
below magnificent snow-capped mountains.
The lake lies at an altitude of 310 metres,
but is so deep that its floor is 89 metres
below sea level. The surface of the water
rises and falls by as much as
12 centimetres every five minutes. According
to Maori legend, this is caused by the still-
beating heart of the slaughtered demon
Matau, whose flexed body made the
Z shape of the lake.

ABOVE AND RIGHT

The Remarkables, Central Otago. *The Remarkables, the jagged mountains on the eastern side of Lake Wakatipu closest to Queenstown, were shaped by the vast ancient glacier that once occupied the lake. The lower slopes of the northern end of the range (right) proved to be good for grazing sheep and one of the pioneers of the district, William Gilbert Rees, was in the early 1860s the first to take up a run here. Rees soon had company and lots of it – in 1862 a couple of his shearers found gold on the banks of the Shotover River, sparking the biggest gold rush the country has seen – and he gave up farming to act as ferryman and supplier to the miners. Around his homestead, The Camp, sprang up the new settlement of Queenstown. At the back of the northern peaks of the range, the three sunny, sheltered bowls of The Remarkables ski area (above), totalling 220 hectares, host skiers and snowboarders of all abilities.*

RIGHT Milford Sound, Fiordland National Park. *One of the iconic images of New Zealand, the pyramid-shaped Mitre Peak (1695 metres) is just one of the elements that makes Milford Sound in Fiordland National Park one of the most popular – and awe-inspiring – destinations in the country. Add towering mountains on all sides descending steeply into the water and hundreds of waterfalls cascading down sheer rock walls and you have the perfect location for a picture postcard. Even the mist and rain that regularly descend on the sound only add to the sense of mystery and wonder. According to Maori legend, the fiords of south-west New Zealand were carved with bare hands by Tu Te Rakiwhanoa, the ancestral hero who shaped the South Island to make it habitable for humans. He started in the south and by the time he got to Piopiotahi (Milford) his fiord technique was so good he created the perfect valley – but it was just too perfect and so the sandflies that have beset visitors ever since were introduced. The more prosaic explanation for the sound is that it is a valley created by ancient glaciers and later drowned by a rise in sea level. Milford Sound was familiar to prehistoric Maori, who braved the cold, wet and sandflies to look for precious greenstone in Anita Bay, and sealers and whalers later used Milford Sound for shelter, but the first permanent settler was Donald Sutherland, 'the hermit of Milford', who accommodated tourists in his hostel from the 1880s.*

LEFT Milford Sound, Fiordland
National Park. *After heavy rain the
waterfalls of Milford Sound run hard and
fast, delighting visitors exploring the fiord in
the fleet of tourist vessels. Milford Sound is
perhaps the most beautiful of the park's
fiords and certainly the easiest to get to. It is
also possible to explore the sound by light
plane or, for the more energetic, sea kayak.*

ABOVE *Milford Sound, Fiordland National Park. High, near-vertical rock faces show how deep the glacier was that carved the valley. The faces continue to plunge below the dark water, all the way down to a sea floor that lies 290 metres below.*

RIGHT *Milford Sound, Fiordland National Park. Dolphins sometimes accompany boats cruising the sound, enjoying a ride on the bow wave and indulging their curiosity about the strange creatures riding above.*

LEFT AND ABOVE *Milford Track, Fiordland National Park. One of the Department of Conservation's 'Great Walks', the Milford Track was once a trail used by Maori in search of greenstone. The walk, described nearly a century ago as 'the finest walk in the world', winds for 53.5 kilometres from Lake Te Anau to Milford Sound. It travels along immense ice-gouged valleys of granite in which beech forest grows beside crystal-clear mountain streams, and over an alpine pass where vegetation is limited to tussock and herbs but the views of the glacial valleys all around are simply spectacular. Much of the track was cut by Quintin Mackinnon, the first Milford Track guide, for whom the high point of the trip is named. The walk is so popular with both locals and visitors from overseas that over summer it is booked out months in advance.*

LEFT *The kea is a large, green parrot that lives in the South Island's high country. It has a reputation as a cheeky and curious bird, hanging around anywhere tourists may offer food. Kea are also known for wanton destruction, and unattended boots, backpacks and cars are all at risk.*

ABOVE   Sutherland Falls, Fiordland National Park. For many years the Sutherland Falls were thought to be the highest waterfall in the world, thanks to the extravagant claims of Donald Sutherland, who discovered it with his friend John McKay. Sutherland estimated the cascade to be 1000 metres high, but surveyors eventually measured it at 580 metres, making it the fifth highest. Lake Quill, from which the water drops, was named after William Quill, the daring young mountaineer who discovered it in 1890 after becoming the first to scale the sheer rock face below.

RIGHT   Bligh Sound, Fiordland National Park. The south-west of the South Island has the highest rainfall in New Zealand – up to 6.5 metres of it every year. The result is that Fiordland, one of the great wilderness areas of the world, plays host to an abundance of life. More than 30 plant species are found only in its wetlands, primeval rainforests and remote mountains. The takahe, a large, flightless bird, was thought to be extinct until it was rediscovered here in 1948, and the rare yellowhead is another resident.

LEFT   Doubtful Sound, Fiordland National Park. South of the more widely known Milford, Doubtful Sound is less visited and thus, some would say, even more beautiful. Sandwiched between the 1200-metre-high Secretary Island and Bauza Island at the entrance to the sound is Te Awaatu Channel Marine Reserve, where adventurous divers who penetrate the surface layer of fresh water discover a unique world of colourful plants and sea creatures.

ABOVE   Lake Te Anau, Fiordland. Boat Harbour, from which launches take walkers to the start of the Milford Track, is at Te Anau Downs, where farmers brave the elements to graze sheep. The largest lake in the South Island, Lake Te Anau sends fingers of water into the densely forested ranges of Fiordland National Park. Also on the western shore are Te Anau-au and Aurora Caves, two huge and spectacular limestone caverns in the Murchison Mountains.

RIGHT   Lake Manapouri, Fiordland. According to Maori tradition, Lake Manapouri was formed by the tears of Moturau and Koronae, daughters of an old chief. Like many New Zealand place names, it has gone through a series of changes: it was originally Rotoua ('rainy lake'), then Moturau (either after one of the sisters or meaning 'hundred islands'), before being accidentally renamed Manapouri by a surveyor. It is now a hydro-electricity lake, although a 1960s plan to raise the water level caused such public outcry that it had to be abandoned.

OTAGO &
SOUTHLAND

Scotland of the South

When the province of Otago was founded in 1853 it included all of the southern third of the South Island. Although Southland soon broke off on its own – only to later rejoin Otago – the people of the two regions share a rugged and hardy spirit and a rich Scottish heritage.

To Maori the southernmost part of the country is Murihiku ('the tail end'), although it is only in Southland that they have retained a significant influence. The name Otago is a corruption of the name Maori gave to the area, Otakou, but the first organised settlement, at Dunedin in 1848, overwhelmed the few Maori that had survived the conquest of invading tribes and the diseases brought by sealers and whalers in the early 19th century. The 'New Edinburgh' was intended to be an exclusively Free Church of Scotland town, away from the church from which the Presbyterians had split and an escape from unemployment.

Although it did not turn out entirely that way, the new town's Scots left an indelible stamp on Dunedin and the region as a whole. In this bottom part of the South Island Scottish place names dominate the signposts and telephone books have dozens of pages devoted to surnames beginning 'Mac'. A little of the accent has even been retained in the Southland burr, with its rolled 'r'.

Dunedin found its feet in the rush that followed Gabriel Read's 1861 discovery of gold near Lawrence, when the population multiplied by five and the city became the powerhouse of the New Zealand economy. Dunedin may have since surrendered its position as the leading city, but it proudly preserves its heritage. Still visible today in this very Victorian city are the ostentatious private homes of the day, as well as a range of impressive public buildings. It also has its modern side – a thriving arts, entertainment and café scene – much of it driven by the students of Otago University, the first in the country and another endowment of the golden years.

The Otago Peninsula is a treasure trove of historic sites, but for many the wildlife holds an even greater attraction. Here, within a short drive of Dunedin, there's a rare opportunity to observe royal albatrosses, yellow-eyed and blue penguins, seals and sea lions at close quarters. In fact abundant wildlife – including all four types of seals found in New Zealand waters – is a feature all along the sandy beaches, rocky headlands and bush-fringed estuaries of Otago and Southland.

The Southern Scenic Route, the 'back way' from Dunedin to Invercargill, sweeps south around the coast through a long neglected part of the country, the Catlins. Beside sparkling streams, lakes and waterfalls in virgin rimu, kamahi, rata and silver beech forests, birds abound – bellbirds, kereru (New Zealand pigeons), fantails, grey warblers and the rare yellowhead. Blow holes, caverns and a 180-million-year-old fossilised forest dot the spectacular, windswept coast and marine wildlife dallies on the shore.

The road leaves behind the huge tracts of towering native forest to enter the very flat, very green and very profitable pastureland of the plain around the main city of Southland, the trim, tidy and well-ordered Invercargill.

Further south still, the port of Bluff is world renowned for its uniquely delicious oysters, which in a meagre season can fetch very high prices and, more prosaically, the great aluminium smelter at Tiwai Point. It is also the departure point for ferries to Stewart Island. Most of New Zealand's third island has been given over to Rakiura National Park, and this great forest of rimu, most of it accessible only on foot or by boat, offers the best chance to see in the wild that most distinctive of national icons, the kiwi.

PREVIOUS PAGES *A lighthouse stands at Taiaroa Head, at the end of the Otago Peninsula.*
ABOVE *The protected New Zealand fur seal, once hunted almost to extinction, is now a common sight on the Otago and Southland coast.*
RIGHT *The 60-million-year-old spherical boulders on the beach at Moeraki, Otago, grew from smaller beginnings.*

PREVIOUS PAGES TOP *Middlemarch, Otago.* In the Strath Taieri plain, Middlemarch has been a farming district for a century and a half, although it took quite some effort to turn the swampy river valley into well-drained fertile farmland. The Otago central railway line made life easier when it reached remote Middlemarch in 1891 and was soon transporting thousands of passengers and even more stock. Today enthusiasts can relive the past with an excursion up the Taieri gorge to Middlemarch on the privately owned line.

PREVIOUS PAGES BOTTOM *Lake Onslow, Otago.* It is not hard to see why pioneering sheep farmers took their flocks to the rolling tussock downs of Otago — even though the winters are freezing and the summers harsh. Lake Onslow, an artificial lake on the Teviot River high in the hills east of Roxburgh, is a popular trout-fishing spot.

LEFT *Otago Peninsula.* The Otago Peninsula reaches out into the Pacific Ocean for about 25 kilometres from Dunedin, forming the southern side of the long, narrow Otago Harbour. Most of the once-forested peninsula is now farmed, but the peninsula also has a diverse range of wildlife, as well as historic places that reflect the intriguing story of the settlement of Otago.

BELOW *Otago Peninsula.* The yellow-eyed penguin is one of the world's rarest penguin species. The hoiho (its Maori name) is a shy creature that nests on the mainland, returning from the day's fishing each evening at dusk. With the development of land for farming, the hoiho became endangered on the peninsula, but now farmers and conservationists work together to provide safe nesting places, and hides from which visitors can view the returning penguins. The hoiho is not the only exceptional creature on the Otago Peninsula: the one royal albatross colony in the world close to human habitation is at Taiaroa Head, and the New Zealand sea lion, the world's rarest, sometimes comes ashore on the beaches.

ABOVE St Clair, Dunedin. *The seaside suburb of St Clair, probably named after the Chapel of St Clair near Edinburgh, has a beach beloved by surfers. New Zealand is an island with a long, much indented coastline, and five of the six largest urban areas are harbour cities. The result is that a high proportion of New Zealanders are, like the residents of St Clair, fortunate enough to live close to the sea.*

MIDDLE Otago Peninsula. *Larnach's Castle is the private fantasy of one of Otago's early European settlers made public. Built in 1871 by W. J. M. Larnach, a businessman who got rich during the gold rush, it is a mismatched arrangement of Scottish baronial parapets, colonial verandahs and classical masonry that was obscenely expensive to build. The tale doesn't end happily: Larnach, who had been dogged by scandal, later lost his wealth and committed suicide in 1898.*

RIGHT Dunedin city. *The municipal chambers preside over the Octagon, Dunedin's central plaza. Completed in 1880, the lavish building is one of many remaining tributes to the city's prosperity during the gold rush years, when it was the biggest city in New Zealand. The name Dunedin, the Gaelic form of Edinburgh, was given by planners creating a 'New Edinburgh', a haven for Free Church of Scotland dissenters from the Presbyterian church.*

LEFT Kaitangata, South Otago.
The Clutha is New Zealand's largest-volume river. From its main source in Lake Wanaka, the 'Mighty Clutha' immediately picks up speed as well as the contents of the Hawea and Kawarau Rivers as it crosses Central Otago (driving hydro-electric power stations on the way) and Otago, divides into the Koau and the Matau (left), and meanders through the fertile Inch Clutha plain to the sea.

LEFT Nugget Point, South Otago.
Nugget Point takes its name from the islands at its base, called 'The Nuggets' by early whalers who couldn't have dreamt of the golden nuggets that would be found decades later further inland. On the exposed promontory fur seals, sea lions and elephant seals bask, while bird life includes yellow-eyed and blue penguins, shags, shearwaters and Australasian gannets.

PREVIOUS PAGES Tautuku, South Otago. In 1839 William Palmer established for
Johnny Jones a whaling station on the Tautuku Peninsula, south of the broad sandy sweep
of Tautuku Bay. At one stage Jones controlled all whaling in the southern part of the
country, and in 1840 he would establish at Waikouaiti the first organised settlement on the
east coast of the South Island, which he ruled as a benevolent dictator, dealing rough justice
as he saw fit. Tautuku Bay is lined with dense coastal podocarp forest and beside the
peninsula an unmodified river estuary empties through the sand dunes.

ABOVE Catlins, Southland. The Catlins district, at the southern tip of the South
Island, is one of New Zealand's least known destinations – yet it has its own wild and
dramatic beauty. Here survival seems to come against the odds – the winters can be brutal
and southerly gales beat coastal trees into a permanent pose of submission – but sea lions and
seals rest on the rocks, penguins nest in the shrubbery, dolphins play in the surf and birds flit
around the the magnificent inland podocarp forests.

RIGHT Slope Point, Southland. The perhaps unimaginatively named Slope Point –
rather than the commonly misstated Bluff – is the southernmost point on the South Island.
Slope Bay was one of many sawmilling settlements in the Catlins that from the 1860s
stripped the ancient forests of rimu, rata and kamahi trees. Fortunately very little logging of
indigenous trees is done today, and 54,000 hectares of forest are protected in parks and
reserves.

FAR LEFT TOP Bluff Harbour,
Southland. *The two arms of the sheltered inlet of Bluff Harbour give it its Maori name, Awarua ('two rivers'). Bluff, 20 kilometres south of Invercargill, is a utilitarian town, with meat processing works and a commercial and fishing port that comes to life every year in autumn with the start of the season for world-famous Bluff oysters. Across the harbour from the town the mammoth Tiwai Point aluminium smelter is the single largest consumer of electricity in New Zealand.*

FAR LEFT BOTTOM Invercargill,
Southland. *At the centre of a highly productive plain, Invercargill is very much a farming service centre. Something of a late developer, the main city of Southland was planned in 1857 with wide streets named after Scottish rivers, and Victorian public buildings like the ivy-covered Southland Boys' High School designed to last for centuries. Despite its location far from the main action of New Zealand life, Invercargill has never conceded a disadvantage, and certainly in the early years of the 21st century the city was booming, with an influx of young people attracted to the free tuition offered by the local polytechnic, and relatively low unemployment.*

LEFT TOP AND BOTTOM
Invercargill, Southland. *The 80-hectare Queens Park, close to the centre of Invercargill, is an example of the thoughtful and forward-thinking planning of the city. It offers a peaceful retreat in its avenues of trees, botanic gardens, rose gardens, bird and animal enclosures and winter garden – and, for those looking to exercise the mind as well as the body, the Southland Museum and Art Gallery.*

ABOVE, RIGHT AND FOLLOWING PAGE *Stewart Island. Unspoiled Stewart Island – the Maori name for the island, Rakiura, means 'glowing sky' – lies across Foveaux Strait from the South Island. Eighty-five per cent of the island is dedicated as Rakiura National Park – from the cliffs, dune lands and wetlands of the west coast, through the impenetrable rainforests, the shrublands and alpine herbfields of the rugged interior, to the sheltered inlets and offshore islands of much of the east coast. Surrounded by the roaring Southern Ocean on three sides, the island is at the mercy of southerly storms yet the few hundred people who live on the island, most of them around Half Moon Bay (above) and Horseshoe Bay (right), still enjoy clear, calm summer days. Many of the residents are direct descendants of original Rakiura Maori and the whalers and traders who settled on the island in the early part of the 19th century.*